THE POWER OF MUSIC

THE
POWER
OF
Music

Pioneering Discoveries in the New Science of Song

ELENA MANNES

Foreword by Aniruddh D. Patel, Ph.D.

WALKER & COMPANY
New York

Published by Walker Publishing Company, Inc., New York

"Whale Sing" by Scott McVay reprinted by kind permission of the author.

All papers used by Walker & Company are natural, recyclable products made from wood grown in well-managed forests. The manufacturing processes conform to the environmental regulations of the country of origin.

LIBRARY OF CONGRESS CATALOGING-IN-PUBLICATION DATA

Mannes, Elena.
The power of music : pioneering discoveries in the new science of song / by Elena Mannes ; foreword by Dr. Aniruddh Patel.
p. cm.
Includes bibliographical references.
ISBN 978-0-8027-1996-6
1. Music—Psychological aspects.   2. Music and science.   I. Title.
ML3830.M19 2011
781'.11—dc22
2010048255

Visit Walker & Company's Web site at www.walkerbooks.com

First U.S. edition 2011

3 5 7 9 10 8 6 4 2

Designed by Adam Bohannon
Typeset by Westchester Book Group
Printed in the U.S.A. by Quad/Graphics, Fairfield, Pennsylvania

TO MY PARENTS

Leopold Damrosch Mannes

and

Evelyn Sabin Mannes

with love and gratitude

CONTENTS

FOREWORD

The power of music to engage human minds and stir the emotions has fascinated thinkers for thousands of years. Well over two thousand years ago Plato remarked that "rhythm and harmony find their way into the inward places of the soul." Despite this ancient interest, it is only in the past decade that an organized community dedicated to research on music and the brain has emerged. The youthfulness of this field partly reflects the new technologies that have spurred its growth, including brain-imaging techniques that allow scientists to observe human brains as they perceive or make music. These remarkable tools have quickly revealed that there is no single "music center" in the brain. In fact, it seems that each subcomponent of music (e.g., harmony, rhythm, etc.) engages a broad network of brain regions, so that music as a whole has access to vast portions of our brains.

This sea change in the scientific study of music has rekindled many old questions about music and the mind. Why does music have such strong effects on our emotions? Is music a universal language? Why does music often make us want to move and dance? How does music get so deeply embedded in our memories? Does learning music improve other cognitive abilities? Can musical activities help restore some of the abilities of neurological patients? These are just a few of the questions that the cognitive neuroscience of music is beginning to address.

One question that has driven much of my own research is: What is the relationship between music and language? In exploring this question, I have found many hidden connections between these two domains. For example, musical and linguistic grammar have many obvious differences, yet research grounded in neuroscience points to significant overlap in the way the brain processes the abstract structure of these two domains. This has opened new ways of studying (and perhaps one day treating) certain language disorders, and illustrates how long-standing debates about music and the mind are being invigorated by new experimental and empirical research.

In her documentary *The Music Instinct*, and now in this book, Elena Mannes has captured a young field at an interesting point in its development. Her film and book give us a portrait of a young research community. Going behind the scenes and beyond the texts of scientific papers, she lets us hear the voices of scientists who are passionate about their research. Adding much more information than was available in the film, this book ranges across many interesting questions about music and the mind, and provides a colorful introduction to a number of current debates in this field.

To those students who may be considering a career in the scientific study of music and the mind, allow me to encourage you. This is a new field and many big questions remain unanswered or only partly addressed. It is a field that allows one to bridge the study of culture and biology, and to develop significant new theories and rapidly connect these theories to experimental studies. Furthermore, there are increasing opportunities to connect basic research with real-world applications of music in education or medical rehabilitation. If you find yourself attracted to this field, please visit the Society for Music Perception and Cognition (www.musicperception.org) to get information on conferences, student opportunities, journals, videos, and other resources for researchers.

The capacity and proclivity for music is one of the most fascinating aspects of being human. As the study of music and the brain expands in this new millennium, prevailing ideas will change and new theories will evolve, but one thing is certain: This exciting journey is now well under way.

Aniruddh D. Patel, Ph.D.,
Esther J. Burnham Senior Fellow, The Neurosciences Institute; president, Society for Music Perception and Cognition; and author of *Music, Language, and the Brain*

Music Matters

*I would teach children music, physics, and philosophy; but most
importantly music, for in the patterns of music and all the arts are the
keys of learning.*

—PLATO

A summer night, an old barn, and music in the air, the melodies and harmonies of amateurs and professionals playing chamber music mingle with the night sounds of crickets
through the barn's open doors. This is how I first knew music:
not as a formal production with remote musicians far up on a
stage, but as an intimate, personal creation joining musicians,
like my father the pianist, and listeners in the experience.

Music is in my genes. The child of a family of professional
musicians, I've always known the power of music. It was all
around me when I was growing up—alive in the house at night,
in concerts, and in recordings. From earliest childhood, I was
aware of my parents' and their friends' passion for this art

form. Music informed our life and the moments that live in my memory. When I now listen to certain pieces, I can still hear the music of that chamber group from my childhood or be transported to my teenage years, driving down a country road with folk or rock music blasting from the radio.

I am not a professional musician, but I've always felt that music is an inextricable, inborn part of me. I have wondered if that's true for everyone, and as a documentary producer/director, I wanted to explore that central question. Within the last decade, there has been an explosion of interest in the science of music, and a new generation of scientists has developed the tools to discover the intimate connections between music and human life. The resulting discoveries reveal hard evidence that music truly is a fundamental aspect of life, something that defines us and binds us together as humans. We are now creating a future in which music will be recognized as a force far more significant than mere entertainment. Some scientists call the potential use of music for healing, changing behavior, and understanding our origins and our universe the stuff of science fiction; imagine prescribing music for neurological disorders and as treatment for the aging brain. Yet our new knowledge offers significant and often startling conclusions about music and the natural world and has major implications for the future of education and medicine.

My fascination with the human relationship to music first led me to develop and produce *The Music Instinct: Science & Song*, a two-hour PBS special, coproduced by New York PBS station WNET/Thirteen that aired in June 2009. The research and production for this project took me on a remarkable journey. I found that passionate scientists all over the world are chasing clues to music's power: Imagine a scientist jiving to the beat of a rock star who's singing inside an fMRI scanner, an archaeologist trekking through a German forest to a remote cave containing the world's oldest instrument, a researcher analyzing the cries of infants lined up in a nursery and finding distinct musical intervals.

The science of music is an adventure happening all around us right now. Neuroscience is delving deeper into the brain to understand its interaction with music. There's new work in genetics and relatively young fields such as psychoneuroimmunology and chronobiology, exploring the complex interplay between music and our being. Every day we are gaining a deeper understanding of this art that so profoundly affects our imagination, our spirit, and our physiology. For centuries, philosophers and musicians themselves have speculated about music, seeking to explain its magic. Yet it is only recently that science has sought in earnest to join the exploration.

We humans know instinctively that music has primal power. Historians and anthropologists have yet to discover a culture without music. Music predates agriculture—and perhaps even language. The foundations of music have been traced as far back as existence itself, to the birth of our universe. Some of the earliest-known musical instruments, crane bone flutes from the Jiahu site in China where humans lived from 7000 to 5700 B.C., produce a tonal scale. Archaeologists in Slovenia recently unearthed a flute that had been fashioned from the femur of a bear by our Neanderthal cousins. These archaic flutes from 36,000 years ago are more than twice as old as the cave paintings in Lascaux, France—and they still create a remarkably pure and beautiful tone.

Singing, along with the use of simpler instruments such as rattles and drums, likely preceded these flutes. In fact, the act of human singing may have begun as long as 250,000 years ago. Even the way young children call their mothers—Ma-ah or Mom-my—is musical, as children use a simple, two-syllable falling musical phrase that appears to be universal across cultures. Children tease one another in a specific, similar, sing-song way no matter where in the world they live.

The elements of music—time, pitch, and volume—echo our pulse, our breath, our movement, and our vocal range. At our emotional core, we experience these elements as joy, sadness, exhilaration, and countless other feelings. Anyone who has been transported by Bach or Mozart, moved to weep by a national anthem or hymn, stirred to dance by a rock rhythm, or transported in time by the notes of a pop tune from the past knows the power of music. And we continually look to music to accompany the most significant moments in our lives, from weddings to wakes. Not only can music be found in every known human society, but there are also surprising common threads that run through all the world's music. A researcher who traveled to a remote corner of Cameroon in Africa where tribe members had never heard Western music found that these tribe members could identify the same emotional qualities in Western music that Western listeners do.[1] This leads us to ask whether there is something about music itself, in the physics of sound and in musical structure, that is universal, bridging time and culture. Language development, human emotion, and intelligence are intimately connected to music. New research on animals and music informs the theory of evolution. Cosmology has contributed fascinating evidence regarding the relationship between musical sound and the birth of the universe.

As I gathered research for the television production, I spoke with visionary scientists and world-famous musicians and it often seemed that I was peeling layers of an onion. Each new study, each new piece of evidence leads to more questions:

- How much of our musicality is learned and how much is innate?
- Can examining the biological foundations of music help scientists unravel the intricate and entangled web of human cognition and brain function?
- Is music, like language, a uniquely human trait?
- Why is music virtually universal across cultures and time— does it provide some evolutionary advantage?
- Could music's role in the natural world reveal a basic bond among all animals?
- Might music contain organizing principles of harmonic vibration that underlie the cosmos itself?
- Can music really make people smarter, happier, and even healthier?

That last question holds the key to the true importance of the new science of music. Sometimes people ask: Don't we already know that music is powerful, that it moves us, that it makes us feel better? Why do we need all these scientific studies? Can't we just enjoy music and accept its mystery just as humans have for centuries?

These questions are understandable. But we're at a moment of breakthrough. This is a profoundly exciting time in music research. We're not just trying to untangle the mysteries of music purely for the sake of knowledge, as wondrous as that may be. What's really significant is that we're learning how music can be more powerful than ever before in human history. And we're learning how to *harness* its power.

Take education. There's been much debate about whether listening to music can make us smarter. But now there's hard evidence that musical *training* can help us learn other skills. And science has led us to the edge of what promises to be a revolution in the use of music for healing. Certainly, music as medicine has been a fixture in indigenous cultures around the world. But in the West, that linkage has been the stuff of myth and fringe science at best. Not so any longer. Many of the scientists I've met came to their work because they had musical training and a love for the art. For example, neuroscientist Jamshed Bharucha trained as a classical violinist. Neurologist and neuroscientist Gottfried Schlaug is trained as an organist. Neuroscientist Daniel Levitin is an amateur saxophone player and former music producer. Each became a scientist in order to answer questions sparked by his musical training. Their passion for music—and for its potential—is driving their work. They, too, know that music may always remain in some ways a mystery. But these passionate scientists clearly see the opportunities that unfold with each new piece of knowledge.

Vocalist/pianist/conductor Bobby McFerrin, pianist and conductor Daniel Barenboim, percussionist Evelyn Glennie, cross-genre violinist Daniel Bernard Roumain (DBR), and British rockers Jarvis Cocker and Richard Hawley are some of the musicians who share a deep curiosity about music with today's leading scientists. Their experiences with music and sound connect hard science to real human experience—interweaving the scientific and the sensory.

Following the story of music has led me from the laboratory to the concert hall, deep into the world of nature, out to the cosmos, and back to the story of our ancestors and their earliest song, and forward to a future of exciting potential. This journey reveals how we understand and experience music, and how it heals the human body and mind. I write not as a scientist, but as a journalist eager to tell a great—and accurate—story, rendering musical and scientific principles and fascinating new research accessible to an interested but not expert reader. My emphasis is on the hard scientific work that underpins the hypothesis that music is inextricably linked to our existence and—if we know how to use it—changes our existence. Sometimes I touch upon so-called fringe science, still in the realm of speculation. But when I do, it is clearly labeled as such. After all, some of this "alternative" thinking might just be paving the way for thorough scientific investigation—just as alternative medicine is receiving some acknowledgment from the world of Western science. One approach does not always negate the other. That said, my passion for this subject is driven by the incontrovertible evidence documented by rigorous science. And I agree with the researchers around the world who believe it's time to take music out of that realm of speculation and wishful thinking and into a new era. One scientist told me: "We have to admit we're still in the embryonic stage of music research."[2] But already the strides have been tremendous.

On a personal level, this journey has led me to a fuller appreciation of my family's musical legacy—and to the conviction that we have only begun to tap music's potential to change our lives.

PART I

The Musical Body and Brain

CHAPTER 1

Feeling the Sound

Do any of us really know what music is? Is it merely physics?
Mathematics? The stuff of romance, or of commerce?
Why is it so important to us? What is its essence?

—STING

Music is the pleasure the human soul experiences from counting
without being aware that it is counting.

—GOTTFRIED WILHELM VON LEIBNIZ,

INVENTOR OF CALCULUS

☫

O ften as a child, I lay in bed at night listening to the sound
of chamber music wafting up the stairs. I also remember
lying under the grand piano, sometimes for a long time, listening and feeling the vibrations of the huge instrument as my father played. It was a physical sensation but it was somehow
emotional, too. I loved it and I felt safe there: connected to
something outside myself, and connected to myself.

Years later, I was amazed to find that several musicians and scientists had memories remarkably similar to mine. Daniel Levitin, cognitive psychologist and neuroscientist, also remembers lying underneath the piano while his mother played. He says he felt enveloped by the sound—mesmerized.[1] Cellist Michael Fitzpatrick recalls that in the third grade he sang a solo from *Carousel*; when he stepped up to the microphone and started to sing "March went out like a lion," he had the sense of putting his fingers into a light socket.[2] And from then on he was hooked on musical sound. Bobby McFerrin, the multi-talented singer/pianist/conductor, echoed a similar childhood experience. He heard his mother playing the piano and he remembers crying. He didn't know why, but he was crying. And he says he's always wondered why it is that music can make us cry so spontaneously.[3]

"It's striking that these childhood experiences of sound are so intense," says McFerrin. It really does make you wonder if we humans have some special physical relationship with musical sound. I can feel that vibration underneath the piano to this day. Did it somehow affect the very cells of my body, cementing the experience into my being?[4]

My musician/scientist father believed that we have a special relationship with music. He addressed the subject in a speech more than a half century ago, long before the current scientific fascination with music. He said:

What I am going to talk about is far from a demonstrable series of scientific facts. In strict parlance, it cannot even be dignified by calling it a theory. In truth, it is at best a series of speculations about music, which has taken place in my mind over a long period of time and which, as a whole, can be called no more than a hypothesis. Since it concerns itself with trying to understand why music is the thing that it is and why it has such a direct and strong impact on the listener . . . I believe that answers to these questions concern themselves basically with . . . the human body.

Leopold Mannes, my father, said that music is fundamentally composed of three elements: time, pitch, and volume. Yet pitch, too, is determined by vibration frequency, so it's really a direct function of time as well. "Time," my father wrote, "forms a sort of space-time continuum, in which music lives, and so . . . time is a very fundamental and compelling factor. I have come to believe," he continued, "that the time or pulse values in music would never have the impact on us which they have, were it not for certain so-called built-in clocks, which we all possess." He identified these "clocks" as heartbeat, the respiratory rate, and the rhythmic movements with which we walk, run, and dance. He then went on to compare these organic rhythms of our bodies to the rhythms of music. For example, marches correspond to the normal human walking rate of 120 steps to the minute—or really a basic 60 rhythm accounting for both legs. And music that is relaxing, my father said, corresponds to the normal resting human pulse of around 84 beats per minute.

Fascinated by music's influence on the human body, I set out to talk to scientists and musicians and discover what they know about the power of music. What is the connection between musical sound and the body? How does it affect the body and maybe even change it?

It turns out that science today is showing that music is in

fact encoded in our bodies and brains. The fact that music seems to trigger our emotions in a way that nothing else does suggests to many scientists that it has an important place in the natural world and that it has something to do with the evolution of our species. Yet the story of the human connection to music begins with our everyday physical reactions to sound.

What is music? In essence, it is vibration. When I speak, sound waves come out of my mouth, compressing air molecules as they travel outward. If you could see a sound wave moving as I speak, you'd observe the molecules come together and then push apart. Think of ripples in a pond. When the body of water is disturbed by a stone being dropped into it or a rowboat pushing through it, waves are created and then the water molecules push back. This back-and-forth movement is the vibration.

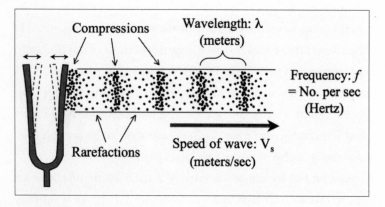

FIGURE 1 Diagram of sound waves created by the vibration of a tuning fork. As the metal ends of the fork go back and forth, they compress the air next to them, causing regions of higher density molecules and slightly higher pressure that move out away from the tuning fork; molecules run into their neighbors in a chain reaction, which creates a progressive wave. When the ends of the fork swing back again, they send out another high pressure region. The distance between the successive pressure peaks is a wavelength and the rate at which these pressure peaks pass a given point is the frequency. CREDIT: MARK WHITTLE

This vibration—this sound—has incredible physical power. A singer's voice, for example, can shatter glass. And sound waves produce patterns in matter. The study of this wave phenomenon is called cymatics, a term based on the Greek word for wave and coined by Swiss scientist Hans Jenny. Jenny expanded on the work of eighteenth-century natural scientist Ernst Chiadni, who spread sand over thin glass plates and set the particles in motion with the vibration of a violin bow. Jenny used different techniques to create patterns in sand and in liquids with vibration. The higher the frequency of the sounds, the more complex the shapes became. Sand was pushed from areas where the vibration was stronger and collected in areas where it was weaker. Jenny showed how different pieces of music create certain patterns. For example, on page 8 is Bach's Toccata and Fugue in D minor, first movement, bar 30.

There's no more telling illustration of the nature of sound—in particular, musical sound—than a very personal one: the story of world-famous percussionist Evelyn Glennie. Glennie grew up on a farm in Scotland, the daughter of an accordionist in a country dance band. Her first instruments were the mouth organ and the clarinet. She has become the first full-time solo professional percussionist in twenty-first-century Western society, and she's done this under very unusual circumstances. Glennie wants to be known simply as a musician, a description she has surely earned. But she knows that what makes her story fascinating is the fact that she has been profoundly deaf since the age of twelve.

Glennie says that the hearing loss was gradual, and now she

FIGURE 2 Cymatics pattern created by Bach's Toccata and Fugue in D minor, 1st movement, bar 30. CREDIT: PHOTOGRAPH FROM *CYMATICS: A STUDY OF WAVE PHENOMENA AND VIBRATION*, COPYRIGHT © 2001 MACROMEDIA PUBLISHING, NEWMARKET, NH, USA.WWW .CYMATICSOURCE.COM. USED BY PERMISSION.

can usually hear someone speaking but can't distinguish the words without the aid of lip-reading. Glennie trained herself to feel the pitches of high frequencies. Of course she was already an accomplished musician. As a child, she had perfect pitch: She was able to identify a note without hearing any related notes next to it. But by the time she was twelve, doctors determined that her degenerative hearing was caused by severe nerve damage and she was now profoundly deaf, with only a little residual hearing left. She has learned to lip-read very proficiently. And her perfect pitch, something she retains although she cannot "hear" a note in the way that a nondeaf person can, helps her to speak.

As a child, Glennie was told she'd never play music again. But she refused to accept that prognosis. When she was twelve, she saw a schoolmate playing percussion and started taking lessons. It "felt right," she says. Her music instructor helped her learn how to feel the music. She would touch the sides of the large timpani (kettledrums). Then the teacher would adjust them to various tones, and Glennie noticed she could sense the different vibrations in different parts of her body. She'd also stand with her hands against the classroom wall to feel the vibrations. Years later, she was accepted by London's prestigious Royal Academy of Music and graduated with honors.[5]

But how can she possibly be a performing musician? How can she hear rhythm and pitch? She showed me how when I went to her home in England. She performed first on marimba and then on an array of percussion instruments. There was no sign of anything out of the ordinary—except that she was playing barefoot. It was like watching a ballerina. Her feet arched and bent and stretched with the music. For Glennie, the fact that music starts with the physical fact of vibration is the essence of her art. "Music is energy," she explains. "It's possible to feel vibrations through the whole body. And for me, this is a very crucial part of what I do." Glennie feels the sound—different rhythms, even different pitches—through her feet and through different parts of her body. She feels the low sounds—like that of a bass drum—in the lower part of her body. And a high sound, like a cowbell, she can sense in the upper part of her body.

Glennie notes that most people tend to make a distinction between hearing a sound and feeling a vibration. But the distinction we make in expressing this difference in English doesn't even exist in the Italian language. The verb *sentire* means "to hear," and the same verb in the reflexive form, *sentirse*, means "to feel." Glennie is convinced that all of us have more ability than we imagine to feel sound with our whole bodies. She points out that we all know what it is to feel vibration when a large truck passes by, and we all can feel the vibration of a bass drum.[6] When I was lying under the piano as my father played, I don't remember making the distinction between hearing and feeling either. So perhaps it's a difference in perception that those of us with "normal" hearing adopt as adults.

Many musicians have an instinctive understanding of how musical sound interacts with our bodies. They know—they feel—that sound impacts our bodies in a way no other art does. Opera singer Irene Gubrud says, "As a very young child, I experienced who I was through sound. I felt whole."[7]

Daniel Bernard Roumain, a young cross-genre violinist who is known as DBR, thinks one reason music is so powerful is that sound actually penetrates our bodies: "You know when someone says that a piece of music 'touched me' or 'moved me,' it's very literal. The sound of my voice enters your ear canal and it's moving your eardrum. That's a very intimate act. I am very literally touching you, and when you speak to me, you are literally touching me. And then we extend that principle to the sound of a violin."[8]

The conductor and pianist Daniel Barenboim believes that our early connection to sound is another reason for its power— one that in today's world we sometimes forget. He thinks that because we live in a very visual society we're more aware of what we see than what we hear. But he reminds us that the latest scientific evidence reveals that the ear, which we now know is active even in the womb, has an advantage over the eye. He also says: "The ear has a head start over the eye, which doesn't see anything until it comes out. The eye is also something that one can control more fully. If you don't like the way I look, and you don't want to see me, you close your eyes and I disappear. But if you don't like my voice and you're in the same room, then you cannot shut your ears in a natural way. Sound literally penetrates the human body."[9]

This human relationship to sound starts early. The fetus begins to develop an auditory system between seventeen and nineteen weeks. Already we are in a world of sound, of breath and heartbeat, of rhythm and vibration. But how do we know what the fetus actually hears? Until recently, there were different theories. Some doctors thought that the fetus could hear only some frequencies, probably high ones. It certainly wasn't known whether we could hear and respond to music before birth until the groundbreaking research of Sheila Woodward, a South African, who wanted to know more about musical sound in the womb. She was a young scientist in the early 1990s—and pregnant; she wondered what music her own child was being exposed to before birth. In her studies at the University of Capetown, she worked with the Institute for Maritime Technology to adapt an underwater microphone so it could be placed in the uterus.

Her team came up with a tiny waterproof hydrophone, about two inches long, that doctors found safe enough to put inside the womb. As part of Woodward's research, this miniature microphone was inserted through the cervix into the uterus of a mother in early labor and placed alongside the neck of the unborn child. The mic recorded exactly what was audible inside the uterus as Woodward played music, sang herself, and had the mother sing. "The big question," she says, "was, 'Does music really exist in the womb and is it very different from the way we hear it in the outside world?'"

As we listen to the recordings that Woodward conducted with several mothers in early stages of labor, we first hear the rhythmic sound of blood coursing through the uterine artery. Says Woodward, "Nature allows us to evolve with rhythm all around us." And her recordings reveal that a landscape of musical sound does indeed surround the fetus. Along with the natural womb sounds, we can hear the strains of a Bach Brandenburg Concerto being played, or the melody of "Mary Had a Little Lamb" as Woodward sings in a normal tone of voice. The recordings show that the very high frequencies, like the sharp attack of an instrument, are attenuated and sound a bit muffled. The overall effect is like listening to music underwater. But when listening to the human voice, one can still detect whether it's a woman or a man. And the tonal quality of the voice comes through.

Just because the sound of music exists in the womb doesn't necessarily mean that the fetus hears it. Yet the "startle response" of the fetus was measured as well, and Woodward's team found that when music was played, the fetal heart rate became slightly elevated. Woodward says it was clear that the fetus reacted, as if to say, "Something's happened and now there's music!"[10] Other studies show that even if only the mother hears music—if she has headphones on, and it is music that she finds soothing—the baby's heart rate lowers while the mother is listening. If the mother finds a certain piece of music stressful, the baby's heart rate goes up. So the fetus is echoing the mother's response to the quality of the music.

Woodward is convinced that we begin learning about music even before birth. She points out that even when music that can penetrate the womb is absent, the fetus is surrounded by those natural rhythms of the body—heartbeat and pulse and breath.[11]

As sound waves enter the ear, they first hit the eardrum, causing it to move in and out. That in turn creates pressure waves inside the cochlea, the snail-shaped, spiral structure of the inner ear. The watery liquid inside the cochlea moves. The cochlea is lined with thousands of tiny hair cells that are also set in motion (see page 1 in the color insert). And, remarkably, hair cells are designed to respond to frequencies from low to high, like a piano keyboard.

The hair cells then convert the vibrations of different frequencies into neural signals, which travel from the ear to the brain stem and up into the brain as electrical signals. And here's something else that I find remarkable: The electrical charge goes to the auditory cortex, which is laid out in *pitch order*. So our auditory system is designed rather like a musical instrument itself, organized to produce our perception of different frequencies.

In a conversation between Bobby McFerrin and Columbia University physicist Brian Greene about the physics of musical sound, McFerrin asked Greene if our very bones and other parts of our bodies can respond to vibration, functioning "like a large ear when we're listening to music." He asked, "Can music get into your pores, like it gets into your ears?" Greene confirmed that since every object on earth vibrates, our bones do too. Greene affirms that the experience of music is something deeply related to our physiology.[12]

Opera singer Irene Gubrud believes without question that "in one sense we are music. Our bodies are a symphony.[13] Cellist Michael Fitzpatrick says, "I think that the deep pulses that the great composers were tapped into are the natural pulse rates of the way our blood flows, the way our heart beats, the way our brain waves flow. And so, when you listen to their music, when it's played with the right intention, it can calm the mind, relax the body, and free the emotions."[14]

But what exactly is *musical* sound? What makes the difference between the sound of a car horn and that of a French horn, between mere noise and music? The difference is in the nature of the sound waves and the ripple they create. A sound we'd consider a noise—like clapping hands or an electric drill—produces a chaotic, irregular sound wave. But a musical note, say a C, is a vibration that's very regular. The wave repeats in an orderly pattern. If you were looking at the air molecules, you'd see a nice cyclical progression: compression, rarefaction, compression. Musical instruments and the human voice—our first instrument—all produce regular sound waves.

Different pitches are produced by variances in the speed of vibrating air molecules. A low note consists of a wave motion that has a long period of time between compressions while a high note's wave has a very short period of time between compressions. Instruments are designed to create different types of sound waves. For example, if one plucks a thin violin string it will vibrate back and forth quickly. And we perceive the sound as a high-pitched note. But a bass has thick strings that vibrate much more slowly when they're plucked. The sound wave that's produced is at a frequency that we perceive as a lower note.

There are mathematical equations that govern how a particular object vibrates, so physicists can predict how a string or wind instrument will sound based on mathematics. These equations for "simple harmonic motion" are what Brian Greene explained in an interview as "the most ubiquitous equations in all physics. They're the ones that we deal with all the time in a wealth of different systems: in cosmology . . . in astrophysics . . . in everyday settings we deal with them. Those equations are the bread and butter of physics."[15] So musical vibration is part of the very fundamentals of what we understand about the universe itself.

Even so, music theorists and musicologists have yet to agree on a single definition of music. Some, like neuroscientist Daniel Levitin, call it "organized sound." That is, if someone has organized sound and called it music, then it is. One aspect of this organized sound is the relationship between tones or frequencies—their intervals. And beyond the physics and math behind the vibration creating a single frequency, there is also math in the intervals.

The Greek philosopher Pythagoras was the first to discover that there is a numerical relationship between certain intervals. When a string is plucked and creates a tone, that fundamental tone actually contains other frequencies within it. These are called overtones and have frequencies higher than the original note—two times, three times, and so forth. The first overtone mathematically is the octave. In Western music that's eight tones above the original note, say C. The second overtone would be a fifth, or five tones, above the octave. The next would be a third above that. That first fundamental tone contains these overtones and more.

This series is experienced whenever we hear a note: We actually hear not just that note, but a series of other tones, or overtones, that occur in a preordained order according to the laws of physics. Some singers can actually produce the overtones within a note so that we can consciously hear them. And there are images of the patterns created by overtones.

Today, German photographer Alexander Lauterwasser is using a new kind of technology to transmit the vibrations of sound and music to water. He's created images showing patterns made by different musical sounds (see page 3 in the color insert, which shows the sound of a monochord with overtone singing).

The same mathematical relationships between tones found in the overtone series also correspond to precise mathematical divisions of a string—the Pythagorean discovery. If we divide a string in half by plucking it, you are playing an octave, a ratio of 2:1 above the original note. Divide the string so that two thirds of it vibrates and you get the fifth, a ratio of 3:2 to the original tone. And if three quarters of the string vibrates, you have the fourth, a ratio of 4:3 to the original tone, and so on (see page 4 in the color insert).

Rhythm, of course, is another quality of music rooted in math, and one that echoes the natural rhythms of the body. The normal resting human heartbeat ranges from 60 to 80 beats per minute for adults. It's not hard to find works that are in sync with this typical heart rate. In fact, examples abound, such as Schubert's Trio in E-flat Major or Mozart's G minor Quintet, introduction to the fourth movement. The pulse of these works feels natural to us. Faster and slower meters suggest either feverish activity or remarkable slowness.

Bobby McFerrin's own music making is intimately connected to his body. He strikes his chest, turning it into a percussion instrument. His great vocal range allows him to become a virtual one-man orchestra, evoking the sounds of various instruments, when he sings. McFerrin *finds* music in the body. He observes that we not only have the natural rhythms of heart rate and breathing, but that we have a rhythm to our gait, and we even brush our teeth in a particular rhythm. I watched McFerrin in the studio as he improvised a piece he aptly named "Walking Pretty Slow"; the only way one could move to that piece is by walking slowly.[16]

My father wrote about the connection between our body rhythms and music more than a half century ago. He cited musical examples showing how certain works follow the built-in "clocks" of our bodies—heart rate and respiration, walking, running. For example, the average walking step, especially when organized as a march, is 120 steps to the minute. "Stars and Stripes Forever" is traditionally played at that rate. Often Brahms's Symphony no. 1, finale is as well. He cited Beethoven's Symphony no. 9, main theme, finale played at 112 as suggesting a comfortable walking rate. And most marches are set to that tempo. Keep in mind that if the tempo is set to 120, the basic pulse is actually given by the first and third beats. So 120 becomes 60. And the normal resting human heart rate is 60 to 80 beats per minute (bpm). *Andante* is a fast walk of 76 to 108 bpm. A fast march might be set at 124 bpm. A musical tempo of lento or largo (slow) is 40 to 60 bpm.

Cellist Michael Fitzpatrick also thinks the great composers were tapped in to the natural pulse rates of the way our blood flows, the way our hearts beat. When you listen to their music, he says, "it has a very specific effect on the body and can calm the mind, relax the body, and free the emotions."[17] And at the frontiers of today's science, researchers have discovered evidence for what many musicians have instinctively felt for centuries.

❧ CHAPTER 2 ❧

Music Plays the Body

The ear is the way.

—THE UPANISHADS

Can you hear the rushing of the river? That is the way.

—ZEN BUDDHIST SAYING

⛥

In a lab, a subject sits before a computer monitor. There's a Band-Aid-like object wrapped around her finger and another device behind her ear, measuring her pulse rate and galvanic skin response—that is, how much she's sweating. First we hear a rather slow, melodic piece played over the speakers—Albinoni's Adagio in G. The monitor shows the readout from the subject. The waves are fairly long and shallow. Then comes the theme from Hitchcock's thriller *Psycho*. The waves quickly become shallower, with sharper spikes. The measuring devices clearly show that the subject has a physiological reaction to the change in music.[1]

A hallmark study on the human physiological response to

music by Robert Zatorre and Anne Blood in Montreal explored whether there is any biological basis for reports of people experiencing "thrills and chills and shivers down the spine" when listening to certain pieces of music. The scientists asked trained musicians to come into the lab and listen to self-selected pieces of music that typically elicited this kind of response from them. While they were listening, the musicians were wired up to test for skin response and muscle tension. They also had their pulse rate and depth of breathing measured. When they listened to passages that caused them to feel a spine-tingling sensation, the monitors showed that their heart rates increased, their breathing deepened, and their muscle tension redoubled. The biological effects were very real and entirely measurable. Music's connection with heart rate, breath, and movement of course means that it can *affect* these bodily functions.[2]

The Cleveland Clinic has conducted studies looking at how music changes heart rate and blood pressure. One study examined how heart rate and blood pressure change relative to tempo. Subjects listened to music samples of different tempos but with the same pitch. The results showed that heart rate went down no matter what the tempo. Normally, when you breathe in, your heart rate goes up, and when you breathe out, your heart rate goes down. That's called heart rate variability. It's one marker of the autonomic nervous system. In a study in which people listened to soothing harp music, their heart rates consistently went down. But their systolic blood pressure (the higher numbers) went up and then down again when the music paused. The researchers were surprised. What was happening was a rhythmicity in the heartbeat that varied with the music. The heartbeat sped up with the music and slowed down with the music.

Other studies showed that a faster tempo raises the heart rate—no matter what the genre—pop, hip-hop, classical, or Indian ragas. So scientists emphasize that we can't assume that all music has the same effect on us. For example, not all music we listen to will be relaxing. Heavy metal or hard rock or hip-hop can actually raise heart rates.[3] The interaction between music and our bodies is complicated and we're just beginning to understand how it works.

Another area of study in current research about music and the body concerns the relationship between music and time. Chronobiology is the science of biological cycles and rhythms. Our bodies operate according to circadian rhythms of upswings of activity alternating with downswings. Some researchers believe our physical and emotional response to music varies depending on what time of day we're listening to a particular piece. If we hear a relaxing piece of music during one of our "up" times it might not seem as relaxing as if we listened during one of our "down" swings.

Yet there's another factor. Music not only echoes our bodies' responses; we echo music. Humans actually *entrain* to a rhythmic beat. This entrainment occurs when there is synchronization between rhythmic cycles. Remember the high school science explanation of this synchronization: Two clock pendulums swinging at different rates eventually swing at the same rate when placed together. The understanding of entrainment, of course, goes back to the seventeenth century when a Dutch physicist, Christiaan Huygens, inventor of the pendulum clock, noticed that two of his clocks on the wall were swinging in perfect synchrony. When he moved them to separate walls, they lost step with each other. This observation led to the theory of coupled oscillators. They're found all over the natural world both within the same organism and between organisms—for example, crickets that chirp in unison. When the oscillators are nonidentical, a strong coupling force can overcome the differences in natural frequency.[4]

I witnessed the principle of musical entrainment at work in a neonatal intensive care unit. A music therapist tapped a wooden gato drum—an African instrument that can mimic the fetal heartbeat. As she continued to tap, the infant's heart rate on the monitor steadied and slowed. It's been noted that Beethoven's String Quartet op. 50, no. 2 uses a pulse just like the fetal heartbeat, mimicking the human heart just like the drum in the neonatal unit.

Music makes us want to move—to tap our feet, to dance. That's entrainment at work as well. Even toddlers will sway and jump to a beat. In fact every known culture throughout human history has incorporated dance just as it has music. Until recently it was thought that only humans have this unconscious entrainment to rhythm. But more on that later.

Scientists have sought to discover if music can affect another physical measurement of stress beyond heart rate and blood pressure—hormones. The chemical messengers secreted from our endocrine system include so-called stress hormones such as ACTH, adrenaline, and cortisol. ACTH, for instance, stimulates the release of adrenaline and cortisol into the bloodstream. Those two chemicals, in turn, affect organs that release stored glucose for energy, increase blood flow to the muscles, and raise blood pressure. This is all in preparation for the so-called fight-or-flight reaction to fear and stress.

The Free University of Berlin conducted a study looking at blood cortisol in healthy individuals exposed to three types of music. They picked a waltz by Johann Strauss for its regular rhythm, a contemporary work by H. W. Henze with a very irregular rhythm, and a piece by Ravi Shankar for its meditative qualities without a strong rhythm. The levels of cortisol were reduced only by the Ravi Shankar piece. The pieces differed in more respects than just rhythm, so it is hard to say definitively that rhythm was the decisive factor affecting cortisol levels. But clearly music had an effect on hormone production.[5]

Other studies have been done in which music is played to patients facing surgery compared to patients in control groups who did not have the opportunity to listen to music. In one, patients were allowed to listen to a type of music of their choosing. The control group heard no music and experienced a large increase in cortisol levels and ACTH levels in the blood. The music group showed a significantly lower level of release of these stress hormones. (Of course, stress hormones aren't always a bad thing; they're intended to give the body extra energy to perform physical tasks when we are in danger.)

In another study, blood cortisol levels were measured in a group of patients, who were further divided into subgroups. One group listened to an hour of music immediately after getting the news that they needed surgery. A second surgical group received no music. And a third group—one that was not getting surgery—was another control. Both of the surgical groups experienced a 50 percent rise in cortisol within fifteen minutes of learning the news. But the music group's cortisol level returned to a normal baseline an hour later, which was equal to the nonsurgical group's levels. So music did reduce the cortisol levels over a period of time.[6]

Music can also be used to *raise* cortisol levels in healthy people. Researchers tested the effects of slow and sedative music versus fast or no music on both trained and untrained runners. Fast music raised the stress hormone levels in the *untrained* runners, indicating that it could be useful to help amateur athletes prepare for strenuous activity for which their bodies aren't already conditioned.[7]

Dr. Barry Bittman, a neurologist and medical director of the Mind-Body Wellness Center in Pennsylvania, has also done a study measuring the effects of group drumming. This preliminary and limited study focusing on cytokines and interleukins (indicators of neuroendocrine and neuroimmune responses) indicated that group drumming may help reverse the stress response. Still, the precise details of the body's complex response demand further research.[8]

And—as Dr. Bittman for one is the first to state—there are qualifications to the cortisol studies. One study showed that cortisol levels change when the subject is sitting as opposed to standing as he drums. So music alone might not be the only factor affecting the levels. Another study that exposed a group to intensive drumming showed that cortisol levels actually dropped even though the subjects were under some stress from the rapid drumming. So cortisol is not the only reliable indicator of stress.[9]

But the decoding of the human genome (the hereditary information of an organism) at the beginning of the century has opened up new possibilities for deciphering music's effect on the body. Cortisol levels and blood pressure used to be the chief available measurements of stress. But they are many steps down the body's chain of reaction to a stimulus. The genome gives a view of exactly what's happening at a molecular level in real time. Dr. Bittman is conducting studies that use genome markers.

Researchers sample subjects' blood for known genomic markers—or "molecular switches"—that trigger biological responses associated with bodily diseases including heart disease, cancer, and diabetes. We'll explore these studies in more detail later, as we examine music and healing. But so far the results indicate that playing a musical instrument can reduce the human stress response at the genomic level.[10]

The genetic research being done on music is part of a whole new field in which researchers look at ways music interacts with our bodies. Psychoneuroimmunology, a fledgling discipline that has emerged in just the last thirty years, studies the interaction between thoughts, feelings, and beliefs and our nervous, immune, and endocrine systems. Our immune and nervous systems are wired through neural circuits in lymphatic tissues. Psychoneuroimmunology is producing results that are very important to the medical and therapeutic uses of music.

There's a sea change in our understanding of how we interact with music. We may have known the mathematical equations behind musical sound since the time of the ancient Greeks, but the math doesn't fully explain what makes music— what makes our *perception* of music—or how we might be able to harness this new knowledge to better our lives. As Brian

Greene puts it, "That gray thing inside our heads plays a role." The ear takes musical sound to the brain and translates sound waves into electrical signals. And indeed, "that gray thing" plays a major and amazing part in the story.

CHAPTER 3

The Brain Plays Music

I think I should have no other mortal wants, if I could always have
plenty of music. It seems to infuse strength into my limbs and ideas into
my brain. Life seems to go on without effort,
when I am filled with music.

—GEORGE ELIOT

W hen we listen to music well, we allow music to happen
to us. We don't think consciously about what's going
on inside our heads. But to actually see the human brain in action as it responds to music is to marvel—both at the phenomenon and at the technology that's allowing us to see it.

Neuroscientist Lawrence Parsons and his technicians ran
a fascinating brain/music experiment. Two British rock stars,
Jarvis Cocker and Richard Hawley, and a hip, shaven-headed
scientist were in an fMRI scanning room. One rocker was
singing in the scanner while his partner strummed the guitar
next to the machine, the music accompanied by the buzz of

the scanner. The control room monitor showed blue-tinted scanner images of the singer's brain; the images constantly morphed and changed with a liquidity that was hypnotizing. As I watched this scene I actually burst out laughing with the wonder and strangeness of what I saw. To Parsons, it was business as usual. But even ten years ago, this event would have been unthinkable.

Only within the last decade has the technology of brain research made it possible to take pictures of the brain in action. Functional magnetic resonance imaging (fMRI) and positron emission tomography (PET) measure changes in the blood flow and blood oxygenation in the brain that indicate neural activity. These new scanning techniques have driven an explosion of research studying the interaction of the brain and music. The results are revolutionizing our understanding of the human connection to music.

In the 1990s, when music science was beginning to take off, the headlines and the literature often focused on one particular question: Are we somehow wired for music? The new brain studies were beginning to offer real proof that we are indeed. Our physical responses to music are rooted in the brain and the way it processes information. There's evidence that we are born with brain structures that allow us to experience music both emotionally and physically. And today many scientists are convinced that there is a biology of music, a hardwired capacity for musical appreciation and expression.

As we learned in chapter 1, the inner ear and the auditory cortex of the brain are built to respond to pitch: The ear converts sound waves to electrical signals sent to the brain, and the auditory cortex is laid out in actual pitch order. Thus, the brain is set up to perceive and process specific pitches—frequencies. The neurons fire synchronously with the fundamental frequency of the sounds we hear. And many scientists believe the brain is also set up to echo the physics of sound.[1]

Some features of music appear to be universal, and there's a physical acoustic reason for this. Our brain has evolved in a world with certain physical regularities. Some neuroscientists believe the brain has incorporated those physical principles in its development.[2] A neuron receives signals from other neurons through connections, or synapses. When these signals reach a certain level, they activate the neuron, which then fires, sending a signal on to other neurons. So when the brain receives an auditory input that includes the fundamental—foundation frequency—of a particular tone, the neurons fire at the same frequency. It seems like a kind of biological miracle.

Neuroscientists like Jamshed Bharucha of Tufts University— a classically trained violinist—predict that researchers will find specific neural cells that are tuned at birth to simple chords— those universal octaves, fifths, and fourths. Other cells might specialize in perceiving patterns of ascending or descending tones.[3]

Perhaps all of us are born musical. Despite having been born into a highly musical family, I've never thought I could sing. All evidence pointed to the fact that even as a child I could carry a tune only if I was singing with others. But science seems to be proving that any deficit I thought I might have had could have been psychological—not built in.

It seems that we all have musical skills to some degree. Dr. Emmanuel Bigand, a French scientist, gave participants in a study musical tests that involved detecting melody, harmony, and large-scale musical structure. The results suggest that differences between musicians and nonmusicians may not be as great as expected.[4] And another study by researchers in England showed that the brains of British adults with no formal musical training and the brains of those with formal training were the same when perceiving simple rhythms.[5] Only a person who has a neurological deficit called amusia is completely unable to perceive pitch.

The key to whether we are born musical may lie in musical memory. Why do we remember songs and melodies? A lot of factors go into those memories—our associations with particular songs at certain times in our lives, for example. But do we have a purely *musical* memory—a memory triggered just by the nature of the music itself? Daniel Levitin devised a test to find out: He asked subjects to sing their favorite songs, and then he compared what they did to recorded versions in the lab, analyzing the pitches.[6] He's analyzed how accurately the subjects replicate tempo and rhythm. It turns out that most people have what Levitin calls "an extraordinary memory for the components of music." We remember tempo just as well as pitch.[7]

And our brain, even without our volition or conscious awareness, does amazing things with music that show just how we are built to perceive the fundamentals of music. Remember the overtone series and those fundamental intervals discussed in chapter 1? Well, if we hear a chord that has all the components of an overtone series except the fundamental note, our brains still "hear" that fundamental tone even though it's not actually there. The brain fills in the missing note.

Neuroscientists are able to pinpoint certain parts of the brain that are involved in perceiving different musical elements. The elements of music include pitch, harmony, melody, loudness, rhythm, meter, tempo, and timbre—the quality of a sound (for example, a violin compared to a bassoon). Let's consider pitch. There are actually neurons that are frequency selective. That is, specific neurons are "tuned" to perceive specific pitches. Some of these neurons are in the primary auditory cortex and surrounding fields. Neuroscientist Robert Zatorre, of McGill University in Canada, finds that the right primary auditory cortex appears to be critical for fine-grained representation of pitch. But his studies show that the processing of pitch *patterns*—that is, melody—requires "higher-order" cortical areas in the frontal cortex.[8] Gerald Langner found areas in the cochlear nucleus and midbrain involved in the perception of pitch and harmony.[9]

Lawrence Parsons, the American neuroscientist now at the University of Sheffield in England, did one of the initial studies identifying brain areas involved in the perception of melody, harmony, and rhythm.

In his first study, Parsons used five musicians and five nonmusicians as subjects. He had them lie in a positron emission tomography (PET scan) machine. A PET scan records blood flow and oxygen levels in the brain, showing what areas are active in response to a particular stimulus. He tested their responses to meter, tempo, and pattern—or melody (see page 5 in the color insert).[10]

The results showed that there are distinct brain areas activated for each of the three musical elements (see page 5 in the color insert). Tempo activated areas in the parietal, insular, frontal, and prefrontal cortex. Meter activated more areas in the left hemisphere and in the basal ganglial and cerebellar areas of the brain. The cerebellum, sitting at the base of the brain, was once thought to principally control movement. Now it's evident that it plays a more complex role. It seems to be involved in coordinating sensory input. Melody (pattern) involved the right and bilateral frontal, prefrontal, parahippocampal, and cerebellar cortices. So Parsons's results for melody or pitch pattern were similar to Zatorre's.

Parsons did find a difference between musicians and non-musicians when it comes to distinguishing pitches. The non-musician subjects needed more support from the cerebellum for this task than the musicians did.[11] Parsons then did a second study using conductors as subjects to look at brain activity for harmony, rhythm, and melody. Again he found that brain activity for each feature of music is different (see page 6 in the color insert).[12]

These studies are fascinating—and groundbreaking—because they are beginning to make it clear how many different parts of our brains are involved in perceiving and processing music. Some of the other brain areas that have been identified as involved in music perception and processing are: the auditory cortex (first stage in the listening process, perception and analysis of tones), the motor cortex (foot tapping, playing an instrument), the prefrontal cortex (the creation of expectations triggered by musical patterns and the violation of patterns/expectations), the sensory cortex (tactile feedback, as in playing an instrument), the visual cortex (reading music), the nucleus accumbens and the amygdala (emotional reactions), the hippocampus (memory for music), the cerebellum (also movement and emotional reactions).

There are even more regions involved in music perception and processing. A remarkable number of events go on inside your brain even if you are only imagining music rather than actually listening to it or playing an instrument. If the music is a march, for example, your neurons are firing in synchronization to the beat. The brain processes all the elements of music—rhythm, pitch, tempo, timbre, etc.—and puts them together in a few thousandths of a second so that we perceive the music not as a collection of parts but as a whole. There are so many different brain areas involved that one can say we have a veritable "brain orchestra" going on inside our heads when we are involved with music (see the color insert).

Researchers used to think that there was a kind of music center in the brain. Today they realize that the whole brain is a music center. Indeed, music probably uses more areas of the brain than any other function. Neuroscientist Robert Zatorre states emphatically that "there isn't a cognitive function that doesn't somehow pertain to music. People have realized that music really does serve as a gateway into understanding human cognition."[13]

Larry Parsons says, "Eight years ago, nobody was studying the brain basis of music. It tells us a lot about the brain at its peak demand—situations that demand the most of it."[14] The growing number of brain studies exploring music processing has informed our understanding of music's impact, illuminating the relationship between rhythm and brain function, the connections between hearing and movement, and the ways in which we process musical tonality.

Petr Janata, a cognitive neuroscientist at the University of California, Davis, has mapped how the tonal relationships of Western music literally "move" through the brain. Now married to a songwriter and very involved with music himself, he studied piano and attended weekly music theory classes as a child. Then, during his teenage years, he explored pop music, listening (unbeknownst to his parents) to the Beatles, Simon and Garfunkel, and the Grateful Dead. He became a true "Deadhead" and to this day retains the air of a rock fan who plays keyboards—no stereotypical academic.

Janata's newest study shows how the Major and minor keys of Western music zero in on a specific area of the brain: the medial prefrontal cortex. An earlier study had shown that this area was active when musicians listen to musical tones. And remember—Western music harmonics are based on that overtone series with its fundamental tones and the specific mathematical ratios between tones. With this in mind, Janata theorized that the geometric relationships between these pitches, pitch combinations (chords), and keys create a kind of tonal space that is represented in the human brain as we process the music. Using brain imaging, Janata set out to prove his theory. He had subjects who were musically experienced undergo several brain-scanning sessions while listening to music. They heard a melody modulating through all the Major and minor keys of Western music. Then the subjects were asked to respond whenever they heard a different instrument and whenever they heard notes that violated the proper key of the melody. In all listeners, the medial prefrontal cortex was activated. And in the scans (see page 7 in the color insert), one can actually see in the brain a representation of the changing tonality and keys. The scans show how certain specific brain structures were activated in many listeners. Janata found consistent activation of certain areas—especially in the rostromedial prefrontal cortex.

Janata identified the prefrontal cortex as the site of what he calls a "tonality map" in the brain (see page 8 in the color insert), which comes from an animation of how music moves around in tonal space. The letters show the twenty-four Major and minor keys. Janata has many images like these—each showing a particular color and activation pattern according to what song is being heard.[15] In a sense, these images are paintings of music in the brain—a clear visual illustration of the concept that "the brain plays music."

The emotions we feel as we listen to music are also reflected in the brain. As Daniel Levitin says, "Goosebumps happen in the brain."[16] The physical changes that music creates in our body—goosebumps, sweat, and shifts in heart rate and blood pressure—are all linked to the brain.

The brain areas activated when we listen to music that we find pleasurable are the same ones activated by drugs or during sex—or as Levitin puts it, "Sex, drugs, and rock and roll right there in the brain." According to him, listening to music also releases neurochemicals such as dopamine, the so-called feel-good hormone; prolactin, the comforting hormone related to mothers breastfeeding infants; and oxytocin, the "trust hormone" associated with sex and bonding with other people.[17]

Pleasurable music may tickle the same brain areas as sex and drugs, but the question is, why does it? Music is not a chemical stimulant like drugs. And unlike sex it's not directly necessary for the continuation of the species. But does it offer some sort of survival benefit? That's the big question driving a lot of the current research. The theory and intuitive answer is that we enjoy music simply because it makes us feel good, influencing our emotions. But theories and intuition don't satisfy scientists. Of course, there is the physical evidence that music creates physiological changes in the body through increased activity of the sympathetic nervous system. That activation indicates emotional arousal when we listen. But neuroscientist Robert Zatorre argues that there is no proof that this emotional arousal is linked to a feeling of *pleasure*. So he and his student Valorie Salimpoor decided to test the theory—and our intuition—that there *is* a link. They wanted to prove a direct connection between emotional arousal (that we can see in the body and the brain) and the subjective feeling of pleasure.

In the study Zatorre and Salimpoor designed, subjects were asked to rate their subjective pleasure states as the researchers measured the sympathetic nervous system responses with real-time millisecond recordings. Music changes constantly as does our response, so this experiment was more "fine-tuned" than previous studies. The results showed that there is a strong correlation between the subjective ratings of pleasure and emotional arousal. Conversely, when participants said they did not feel pleasure, there were no great increases in emotional arousal. It's interesting that while the subjects may all have been entraining to the tempo of the music, different people had different physiological responses depending on how pleasurable they found the piece. Entrainment alone didn't lead to pleasure.[18]

Studies like these, probing the details about how our brains interact with music, have a big-picture importance that goes far beyond the fine points of each specific finding. There's a remarkable synergy between music and brain research just because music involves so many parts of the brain. Thus, as the brain teaches us about music, music is teaching us about the brain. It's startling to realize that even ten or fifteen years ago, we knew far less about the human brain than we do today. Neuroscience remains uncharted territory to a large degree—one of the "last frontiers" in science, as Daniel Levitin puts it.[19] Robert Zatorre reminds us that "until a few years ago, people thought of music as a cultural activity, but not as something that was valuable to study scientifically."[20] It strikes me that the brain mapping under way around the world through music/science research is probably one day going to seem like the product of early cartographers trying to give accurate pictures of the globe.

Neuroscientists are now moving into a fascinating new realm of investigation. They've begun to go beyond the study of individual brains; they're looking at how our brains interact when we do music together. Do they synchronize to the music and to each other?

Larry Parsons did the very first experiment using brain imaging to see what happens when two musicians play together. It was the study with British rockers Jarvis Cocker and Richard Hawley. Parsons had Cocker in the fMRI scanner singing while Hawley sat next to the scanner playing guitar. All of the brain-imaging studies done before this one looked at a single person's brain during a single musical experience. Parsons set out to see the brain areas involved in what he terms "social, pair-wise musical performance."[21]

Both musicians were really eager to do the experiment. Hawley facetiously commented that "we're both curious to know whether we have any brain left after many years in the music industry. When you write songs and stuff like that, you don't really know where they come from. And so it's kind of interesting to find out what's going on in your head."[22]

Parsons did scans of Cocker while he was singing alone to compare to the ones taken when he sang along with Hawley's guitar. When he analyzed the scans, Parsons found that compared to when he sang with Hawley playing, Cocker's brain was more active in areas for phrasing and coordinating music as well as in the areas associated with cognitive and emotional interaction. What Parsons saw was the brain doing "complicated social work with a lot of millisecond decision planning" as the musicians performed. He was also looking at the brain at its peak demand, when two musicians or singers are working together to create music. What this pioneering study shows is that "music is intrinsically social," as Parsons says.[23]

Other researchers are very intrigued by the idea that music can actually synchronize people's brain states. When we go to a concert—be it rock or classical—part of what makes it enjoyable and special is that it's a *shared* experience. And it's not just that our physical bodies are present in the same space. We're all entraining to the beat. So do our brains synchronize in other ways, too? Can music put a community—a society—of

brains into the same state? Logic says yes. And some researchers believe that the field of music neuroscience is now moving
from the study of individual brains toward the study of a society of brain states.

❧ CHAPTER 4 ❧

Is Music
Our Genetic Birthright?

Without music life would be a mistake.

—FRIEDRICH NIETZSCHE

▼

Music—figuratively speaking—is in *my* genes. I grew up with it all around me. I was exposed constantly to the melodies, harmonies, and form of Western classical music. But what about other genres? Do I have the same natural affinity for other kinds of music, for the music of other cultures? Or am I able to appreciate only the music I grew up with, and unable to experience pleasure listening to music that is quite different from what I'm used to?

The answer is that at least some of the time, enjoying unfamiliar music is difficult for people. Take me to a Chinese opera and I'm pretty eager for the end—not because I don't respect this music but because I don't "get" it. I don't understand what

40

the composer is doing and I'm not moved emotionally. It's like not being able to speak a foreign language.

If we are really "wired" for music to some degree, if our brains and bodies are built to perceive and respond to music, how do we explain differing responses to different kinds of music? Why are there differing musical systems among various cultures? Why does Asian music use a pentatonic—five-note—scale while European music uses an octave—seven-note—scale? Why don't some cultures in the Middle East, for example, associate minor keys with sadness, as their Western counterparts do? To what degree is music universally built into us, and to what degree are musical tastes and responses shaped by our culture? What we've learned about how we process music leads to the great and fascinating debate of nature vs. nurture, biology vs. culture.

Musician Bobby McFerrin asked neuroscientist Daniel Levitin about this very issue. He wondered what's going on with the neurons in our brains if they're "wired for music" yet we respond in a special way to music of our own culture. "Does that mean that the neurons or whatever is working in your brain become accustomed to hearing something in a certain context? They're free in the beginning, right?" he asked Levitin.[1] They are "free in the beginning," Levitin confirmed.[2] So then what happens over time? McFerrin asked. "To hear a particular kind of music with all its structures, are the neurons fused in a certain way to accept this music in a particular understanding?"[3]

The answer is that we're born with some thirty billion neurons that are a canvas for learning. It's true that neuroscientists do pretty much agree that our brains come wired for music to some degree. But the connections between neurons are also shaped by experience. As Levitin explained, "The process of maturation in the human child is a process of hooking those neurons up into neural circuits, neural networks. We're all born with a music module that allows us to learn the rules of whatever music we're exposed to."[4]

But this is only the beginning of the debate about biology vs. culture. And the more we learn about how the brain interacts with music, the more heated the discussion.

Neuroscientist Jamshed Bharucha is trained as a classical violinist, steeped in the mores of Western music. But as an Indian, he is also intimately familiar with that culture's music. However, for most people—even most musicians—accustomed to Western classical music, it's hard to decipher the patterns and structures of Indian music. We find it hard to follow the "story" of the music. And our emotional response is muted—or silent. An Indian raga can draw tears from an Indian listener but no response from a Western audience.

Bharucha is convinced biology is the reason that culture changes the way we hear. "The brain is capable of an extraordinary amount of learning," he said. "And learning takes the form of actually changing the biology. It really changes the connections between neurons in the brain so that as we have grown up in a culture we actually come to the perceptional situation with different machinery."[5]

That comment sparked a friendly argument with psychologist Sandra Trehub from the University of Toronto. Trehub's specialty is the study of how babies and toddlers respond to music. She wondered if infants can recognize certain musical intervals. And some years ago she designed some pioneering studies to find answers. She exposed infants to melodies or patterns that were either consonant or dissonant. Consonant combinations of notes are smooth-sounding intervals. Dissonant combinations are two notes next to each other sounded together that sound "rough" or discordant—intervals that seem to "clash," like the beginning of "Chopsticks"—two notes next to each other sounded together.

Trehub used classical psychological testing to record what drew and held the babies' attention. An infant was held on the mother's lap in a soundproof booth while different melodies are played one at a time on two monitors to the left and the right. There was a neutral video image on both monitors. Trehub and her assistants videotaped sessions and analyzed the babies' responses to one monitor—to one melody—or the other. The results clearly showed, Trehub says, "that babies could detect very tiny differences if what they were listening to initially was a consonant pattern. In other words, they noticed dissonance as a contrast."[6]

Other researchers then went on to examine what infants *preferred*—consonance or dissonance. And they found that if the babies had a choice, they spent more time listening to the consonant music.

Recently, there has been work by Trehub herself and by biologist Josh McDermott, indicating that the preference for consonance may be at least somewhat due to learning. One study by McDermott found that older subjects with musical training had a stronger preference for consonance.[7] Sandra Trehub decided to test what would happen if she played atonal music to infants compared to more melodic selections. She did the experiment with both six- and twelve-month-old babies and found that actually they didn't mind the atonal music that many Western adults find jarring. It seemed to make no difference to them. She continued testing and found that the six-month-olds continued to be indifferent. But she did find that the year-old babies showed a moderate "preference" actually for the atonal. It was something different, so they paid attention. Trehub points out that in scientific terms, "preference" doesn't mean they liked it. It just means they listened a bit longer to the new-sounding music. She says these new studies don't negate her earlier research showing a preference for consonance, but it does mean we need to clearly understand what preference means. And these studies, like McDermott's research, indicate that some of the preference for consonance could be learned. Some cultures, Trehub points out, like dissonance. The gamelan, a Balinese instrument, is naturally dissonant because of the way it's tuned. And the Balinese actually accentuate the dissonance because they enjoy it. So a Balinese baby most likely would learn more of a preference for dissonance than a Western baby, even assuming an inborn attunement to consonance.[8]

Sandra Trehub still believes that we're "wired" to some degree to respond to those smooth-sounding intervals. Maybe that means we then learn them more easily. The cultural exposure to a musical system that uses them may reinforce them.[9]

Laurel Trainor, a psychologist at McMaster University in Ontario, did the study showing infants prefer consonance.[10] But she points out that there are two kinds of consonance. One is a sensory consonance; that's for isolated intervals when the subject hears two or three notes together. The other is musical consonance and depends on the context. For example, Trainor explains, "You can take the C Major key and suddenly play a G-flat Major chord and it will sound dissonant because it won't fit in that context. The same chord in another context would sound consonant." Trainor believes that even an early response in favor of consonance could be learned to some degree.[11]

But Sandra Trehub still believes that biology ultimately trumps culture and that we come into the world wired to respond to certain musical intervals—the smooth-sounding consonant ones, some of which are those first intervals in the overtone series, the low-number, simple-ratio intervals found in the music of most cultures—the octave, the fifth, and the perfect fourth. A Major third in Western music—say a C Major triad C, E, and G—is also consonant.[12] Think of the opening notes of "Here Comes the Bride."

Some people say the fetus could hear and "learn" these intervals in the womb, from music the parents play. But a study by a Japanese researcher of hearing babies born to deaf parents showed they too had a preference for consonant, smooth-sounding intervals,[13] although Sandra Trehub is convinced the exposure of these babies in utero to music of this description would have been extremely limited. So, to her, that Japanese study is further evidence that there really is an inborn preference for those smooth-sounding consonant intervals. And furthermore, she says it builds the evidentiary case that "our auditory system is designed in such a way that certain things are going to sound more pleasing than others."[14]

And is it possible that we start forming our musical preferences even before birth? Kathleen Wermke, a researcher at the University of Würzberg, works surrounded by infants. They're her specialty. She noticed that the cries of babies seemed to have music-like intervals. So she decided to analyze them. In her lab, she recorded infants' cries in an audio booth. Then all the data was carefully analyzed, measuring the intervals of the baby sounds. "We found out that they sound extremely musical," Wermke says—still surprised. "We said, 'Oh, this is really astonishing because nobody thought that small babies might cry in musical intervals.'"[15]

She showed me the corresponding graphs measuring the intervals visually according to frequency, as we listened to the cries on the computer. I could see the intervals—the fifths, fourths, and thirds. When the baby cries are slowed down, one can clearly hear the intervals. Musicians were brought into the lab to listen to the cries and confirm the computer analyses. Wermke found that these intervals occur in the baby cries far more often than could be attributable to mere chance. Remember, too, that those simple-ratio intervals are built into the physics of sound—the harmonics of a vibrating string or other instrument.

Kathleen Wermke also found many *minor* thirds in the babies' cries. Think of children teasing each other in the familiar singsong way they do no matter where in the world they live— that "nyeah nyeah n'nyeah nyeah" chant. That's a minor third—"nyeah, nyeah." It's also called "the mommy sound"— the one that demands immediate attention! *Ma-a-ah M-ee.* Many musicians believe the minor third also is related to the harmonic overtone series.

One researcher has shown by taking ultrasounds of fetuses that there's a selective response to familiar songs even before birth.[16] So it seems that they're actually learning the songs and reacting to them in the womb.

Still, there's also recent evidence that infants *can* learn the music of their particular culture very early—even earlier than we imagined. Even if infants do show a preference for consonant intervals in isolation—sensory consonance—it's known that they don't care about musical key while adults care a lot. Adults notice if a note doesn't fit in the key. Laurel Trainor wanted to see how early infants might be taught scale structure and tonality. She took two groups of infants between six and twelve months of age. One was exposed to active music making for six months. They took a Suzuki-based early music class in which they learned to play songs, play drums, and perform rhythm exercises. The other group was a passive-listening class. The infants didn't actively engage in music; the music was just playing in the background.[17] At the end of the six months, Trainor gave both groups preference tests. And the results showed the infants in the passive group didn't care whether they heard tonal or atonal (music that didn't fit in the Western scale system). The infants in the active group, however, showed a preference for tonal music. So Trainor concludes that "what that demonstrates is that you can train active music participation starting between six and twelve months of age. They will actually learn scale structure. So experience plays a huge role in wiring up the brain."[18]

Are we born with an innate sense of rhythm and pitch? Evidence of inborn musical ability continues to build. A very recent study regarding rhythm shows we learn the elements of music earlier than previously assumed. A team of Hungarian and Dutch researchers demonstrated that two- to three-day-old babies can detect the beat in music. Beat induction, as it's called, is what allows us to clap, make music together, and dance to a rhythm. This joint European study challenges the idea that we learn beat induction only in the first few months of life. Instead, the new research shows that either it must be innate or learned in the womb since the fetus has auditory capability about three months before birth. The researchers used scalp electrodes on newborns to measure electrical brain signals. They played the babies a simple rock rhythm with hi-hat, snare, and bass drum. Then they played simple variants of the basic rhythm—like missing the downbeat. And the babies' brains actually produced an electrical response after each deviant rhythm, indicating they expected to hear that downbeat in the regular place.[19]

Remember, too, that connection between the rhythm of the human heartbeat and much of the world's music. The normal heartbeat ranges from 65 to 80 beats per minute. And rhythm patterns in all societies—from primitive drumbeats to the symphonies of Mozart—tend to stay within the heartbeat range of 60 to 150 beats per minute.

The question as to whether we are born with an innate sense of pitch brings us to the fascinating topic of *absolute pitch*—also called perfect pitch. Many people wonder if all great musicians have absolute pitch. And why don't all of us have this ability to identify a musical tone in isolation—that is, without hearing other tones around it? Well, first of all, one doesn't need perfect pitch to be a good, even great, musician. Furthermore, the science shows that we probably all do have absolute pitch when we're born, but then most of us lose it.

Diana Deutsch, a neuropsychologist at the University of

California, has done extensive research into perfect pitch. She has speculated that the skill—or at least the ability to retain it—may be related to how much we practice it as we mature. In tonal languages like Mandarin Chinese, pitch is very important. The meaning of a word can depend on the pitch. So Deutsch did a survey in Beijing. She found that the Chinese have a remarkable facility for perfect pitch. But maybe it was just genetics and not culture that accounted for this unusually high number of people with perfect pitch. To explore that possibility, she also examined three groups of Vietnamese in California. One group had emigrated as adults, one had arrived at an early age, and another consisted of people who had been born in the United States. The first two groups had a higher prevalence of absolute pitch. So the theory is that if we have inborn perfect pitch, we are likely to lose it if we don't speak a tonal language.[20] Other researchers have done studies also showing that absolute pitch diminishes in the first several months of infancy.[21] So these results seem to confirm the theory that "if you don't use it, you lose it."

Sandra Trehub makes another point to support the argument that at birth our biology predisposes us to respond to musical universals no matter what culture we're born into. She reminds us that while there certainly are big differences between the musical systems of different cultures, that's really only true when it comes to "art" music. When we get away from the highly structured classical forms of each society and listen to types of music familiar to *every* culture—like lullabies—it's a different story. All lullabies have a narrow pitch range, falling pitch contours, and they're quiet and very repetitive. Listen to a lullaby from Bangladesh and it's true: We can recognize it as a lullaby and hear that it is fundamentally the same as a song we'd sing to an infant born in the West.[22]

Music *itself* is common—used across time and culture to bring people together, to lead them in prayer, to lead them to war, to feed romance, and to ease broken hearts. But in this biology vs. culture argument, ethnomusicologists—the specialists in music of different cultures—insist we simply cannot say that there are significant common elements in the music of all societies. Ethnomusicologist Kay Shelemay, of Harvard, explained to me that whereas "a neuroscientist is really looking at the hardware [and to a certain extent the software] of music cognition, the ethnomusicologist is more concerned with process, and how that hardware and software are used to really make sense and interact with the world." She and others in the field want to learn "how music operates in the world—on the very boundary of culture and cognition." On that boundary, ethnomusicologists look for—and find—great differences between the musical systems. They want to understand music, Shelemay explains, "as a cultural phenomenon, the ways in which music helps construct environments, the ways in which it lends meaning."[23]

Kay Shelemay warns that we must be careful when we talk about musical "universals." No one disputes that the octave is universal. But even the fifth and fourth that occur in most music are not completely universal, Shelemay argues. Furthermore, in some musical systems, there is no concept of harmony—the vertical construction of intervals as chords, for example. There may only be a horizontal line akin to what we in the West call melody. And sometimes there's not even melody as we think of it. She gives as an example the Ethiopian musical tradition from the Ethiopian highlands. There's no concept of music as individual pitches. Music is learned and performed in association with sacred texts, in small phrases—each associated with a verse and not thought of as melodies constructed from pitches. Ethiopian music—like Balinese music—has tuning systems and systems of pitch organization that are different from Western music.[24]

Cultural music traditions were illustrated when Bobby McFerrin worked with singers from several cultures for *The Music Instinct* television program. One singer from the Middle East demonstrated the microtonal system. The interval of a third, for example, is different—smaller—than either the Western Major or minor third. Westerners listening to her probably think she's out of tune.

Shelemay insists that "Western notions of melody and harmony are exactly that—Western notions of melody and harmony." And even if music *sounds* the same, she says, it might come from a different impetus or intent; it might carry a meaning unique to its culture.

Still, lullabies and some other forms of music do exist worldwide across culture and time. Laments are another example of musical forms that cross cultural boundaries. Shelemay says laments are very common, "perhaps because sadness, loss, grief are a given of human life." And she acknowledges that musically they share a characteristic: They sound like crying.

Bobby McFerrin has traveled around the world performing with musicians from many different cultures. "There are boundaries like country to country," he says, "but all you have to do is walk across them. As soon as we play or sing together, we can easily find ways of identifying each other, who we are and what our stories are through music without uttering a single word. You know, music does that."[25]

Daniel Bernard Roumain (DBR), a Haitian American cross-genre violinist and composer, finds commonality between hip-hop and Mozart. DBR pointed out that often hip-hop composers are actually sampling Mozart or Beethoven or other classical music. And, in turn, "Mozart used Turkish melodies in his music; Beethoven used music from other countries in his music—from Spain and even France. So there's a tradition among composers of using folk music—sampling, if you will, from other countries, other cultures, other disciplines even, and incorporating that into their music."[26]

In the biology/culture debate, one experiment by Tom Fritz stands out in its simplicity and for its remarkable result. Fritz was a researcher at the Max Planck Institute in Leipzig, Germany. He realized that there were some questions in the study of music that fancy scientific equipment like fMRI machines cannot answer. What is it in music that is universal? And what is it that has an effect on us through cultural imprinting? So Fritz went on a quest.

He organized a research trip in 2005 to a remote area in Africa—north Cameroon in the Mandara mountain range. This is home to a tribe called the Mafa. It's one of the rare regions in today's world where one can find people never exposed to Western music—not on an iPod, not on a computer, not even on a radio. They don't even go to the market or to a church where they might have listened to some other culture's music. Fritz knew that the Mafa people had never in their lives heard Western music.

The Mafa do have their own music, but they don't call it that. They have no word for music. But everyone sings. And they play on a kind of flute or horn made of iron and some special wax. They exhale continually for hours, producing tones from these instruments. The sound is harsh to our ears—discordant and jarring.

Fritz designed a simple experiment to do with the Mafa. He decided to show them faces depicting different emotions: happy, sad, and scary. He had them listen to pieces of Western music with headphones. And then he asked them to point to the face they thought represented the emotion they heard in the music. Remember, these tribe members had never before heard Western music—no symphonies, no piano music, nothing. Fritz was asking if someone who has never in his or her life heard any kind of Western melody could still understand the emotional meaning of the music. And the answer would tell something about why we respond to Mozart or Beethoven—or Taylor Swift or the Black Eyed Peas. If the Mafa responded as we do, must there be something inherent in the melody that evokes that response rather than something we are culturally imprinted on by our music culture history?

Fritz did this experiment with many people over the weeks that he lived in the mountain village with the Mafa. He played them Western piano music—specially composed and tested with Western listeners to test the ability to recognize happy, sad, and fearful emotions.[27]

He collected all the responses and carefully recorded them for analysis. The data clearly demonstrated that the Mafa's ability to recognize musical emotions was much better than chance for all three emotional states. For example, by chance alone they would probably identify "happy" music a third of the time. But the Mafa picked it correctly 60 percent of the time on average. And they were right about the other two emotions about half the time. The scores weren't as high as Western listeners scored with the same music. But still, given the Mafa's total inexperience with the Western musical system, the results were remarkable.

Fritz believes that his experiment shows there's no doubt that music is a key part of what makes us human. "Basically it's a simple answer," he says. "The emotional expression of the music is inherent in the music itself and not solely decodable through cultural imprinting."[28]

I personally found it very moving to see the footage of the Mafa with headsets on, listening to a kind of music, a kind of sound they'd never heard before—and actually *feeling* what our music—from worlds away—was trying to say. To me, that's evidence that weighs heavily on the nature and biology side of the nature/nurture debate.

Culture surely helps shape the way we hear music. The structure of the sound, the way all those elements of pitch, rhythm, timbre, and so forth are combined to act upon our brain and our emotions in a particular way do vary in different cultures. But then there's Tom Fritz's study. The Mafa had never heard Western music but still decoded it emotionally. And if a newborn, presumably never exposed to Western music, still responds to those consonant, simple-ratio intervals, it seems to me to indicate that our biology and some basic elements of musical sound fit together in all human beings—that music, at least to some degree, is bred into us.

PART II

The Musical Self

⊰ CHAPTER 5 ⊱

Agony and Ecstasy:
How We Listen

*When I hear music, I fear no danger, I am invulnerable, I see no foe. I
am related to the earliest times and to the latest.*

—HENRY DAVID THOREAU

ᛏᛉ

If we listen—really listen—to music, we recognize moments
that give us a little start, a shiver down the spine, a frisson of
surprise. It could be a chord change or a harmony or a turn in
the melody. And then a song or a phrase may elicit a memory
and a particular emotion. For example, when I hear a Joni
Mitchell song or Joan Baez or of course the Beatles, I am taken
back to my room as a teenager or my first car or a person I was
with when I heard these pieces of music. So when music makes
us feel something, how much is due to our associations with it
and how much is due to something in the music itself? Are
there certain elements built into the musical structure of

songs and symphonies and sonatas that naturally and automatically elicit emotions from us?

These are questions that fascinate researchers like cognitive psychologist John Sloboda, who is also a trained singer. He remembers his reaction to a piece that first got him hooked on music at the age of five. It was part of the *Nutcracker Suite* by Tchaikovsky. He begged for piano lessons after this early exposure. Now, at Keele University in England, Sloboda conducts studies focusing on how we actually engage with music: How do we extract certain elements? How do we make sense of it? For example, he asks people to identify moments in music that elicit specific bodily responses usually associated with emotions—such as tears. Then he analyzes the qualities of those musical moments across the data he's gathered. His results link certain musical devices to certain emotions. A musical device called an appoggiatura often elicits tears. This musical device has elements of surprise. An appoggiatura is a dissonance, or a clash in the harmony. And it resolves to something smoother: One note moves down a step in the scale. A famous example is the first theme of Albinoni's Adagio for Strings, which contains three appoggiaturas in the first eight notes. In the David Willcocks harmonization of the Christmas carol "Hark! The Herald Angels Sing," one chord is reharmonized in the last verse to create an unexpected dissonance that gives an emotional thrill and often tears to the eyes. As Sloboda points out, "It's the tension, release, tension, release, that almost rocking feeling that seems to cause tears to well up in a lot of people. It is," he adds, "about expectations not fulfilled, which is very often the basis of any emotion. We feel strong emotion when something happens not as planned."[1] Sloboda notes that composers frequently break formal rules to create the element of surprise.[2]

The movement of tension and release is fundamental to the Western system of tonality and the basic intervals built into that system. The music "comes home" to the root note or basic harmony of a key after moving away. For example, in the Western musical system, a chord built on the root of the scale is called the tonic. So take a C Major chord C, E, G. A melody might depart from that chord, but when it comes back to it, the listener will feel resolution.

What about, say, Chinese music? There's probably the element of surprise in music of other cultures. But the research needs to be done to prove the effects of structural devices in the music. In Western music, we know that appoggiaturas, for instance, occur in all types of music from Monteverdi operas to Bach to the Beatles.

There are other musical devices that can give us that shiver down the spine or cause the hair on our arms to stand on end. Take the enharmonic change—a fancy word for a particular type of change in harmony under a melody note that stays the same. When there's a chord with a particular note in it and then the composer creates a new chord around the same note but with a different harmony, that's an enharmonic change. Sloboda cites the example of the twentieth-century composer Arnold Schoenberg's *Transfigured Night*. Schoenberg transfigures an E-flat minor chord to a D Major chord around the same note (G-flat–F-sharp).

And then there's something we probably are all familiar with whether we know it or not—rhythmic syncopation. Sloboda talks about it as "when something really major happens when you're not expecting it." Syncopation means that there's a stress on a beat that's usually unstressed or a rest where one would expect a stress. The expected rhythm is interrupted.

While we think of syncopation as occurring in pop and rhythm and blues music (for example, the classic Bo Diddley rhythm), it occurs in classical music as well. For example, there is a section in the last movement of Beethoven's Fourth Piano Concerto that has a repeating four-square rhythm—1-2-3-4—with the accent on the first beat. Then it misses a beat so that a main beat happens before you expect it. The syncopation gives us that little start and makes us want to move, to dance. It energizes us and actually raises the heartbeat, Sloboda points out.

In the study described above, Sloboda asked people to identify different pieces of music that had particular effects on them—a feeling of chills down the spine, hair standing on end, or increased heart rate. About 30 percent of the subjects actually could do that. Then he studied the works they chose. They usually didn't pick the same pieces of music. But the ones they chose did have in common certain structural devices. And those structural devices create surprise by violating the patterns of music. People like predictability. But they also like when the rules are then broken. Appoggiaturas, enharmonic changes, and syncopation are all "tweaking" our neurons by taking detours off the expected road map. As a result, they shift our emotions as we listen.[3]

There are now brain-imaging studies that show how musical structure works on the brain. Neuroscientists Daniel Levitin and Vinod Menon did a study along with Stanford music professor and composer Jonathan Berger observing how the brain responds during a transition between movements in a classical symphony. The music might slow down in tempo or go through a change in intensity in preparation for a structural change. It's a kind of pause, like a paragraph or breath after a spoken sentence. The subjects listened to sections of symphonies by the baroque composer William Boyce while lying in an fMRI scanner. What happened was that the ten-second window to the musical transition triggered what Menon called "a flurry of neural activity."

The brain was anticipating the end of a section of the music. The scientists found it significant that the peak of neural activity occurred during the *silence* of the transition. This suggests that the silence is what helps the brain to decode musical structure, making sense of what might otherwise be "a continuous stream of undifferentiated information."[4] Menon said, "Sound is very good at setting up anticipation, music in particular. If you listen to the great composers, they were masters at setting up silence and using expectation violation to make their masterpieces." As a musician, Berger found the importance of silence unsurprising: "It is during the space between the music, during the silences, that we set up networks and process all this information. From a musician's perspective, it all makes sense. It's all about expectation."[5]

Musicians know very well what musical surprise is all about. British rockster/songwriter Richard Hawley said that when he composes, "I know the mechanics of music, you know, chords and how it all fits together. I sort of worked the theory out with my grandfather and my dad. And they showed me—this is C, you know, that's F and G and they're the three main chords in that key and you get the related minors—D minor, E minor.

But you can come up with melodies that completely break all those rules sometimes."[6]

Other work with brain imaging by neuroscientists confirms the effect of surprise by recording how violations of listeners' expectations create changes in brain activity. Stefan Koelsch did a study at the Max Planck Institute in Leipzig, Germany, in which he looked at brain activity when listeners heard irregular chords—that is, chords not expected within the tonal structure of the music. He played a normal version of chords in a Bach chorale and then a version with a harmonic sequence ending in an irregular chord. Koelsch found that the irregular chords do cause changes in the brain—specifically in the orbital frontolateral cortex and the medial inferior frontal gyrus. Both areas have been shown to play a role in the evaluation of the emotional importance of a sensory stimulus.[7] The amygdala is known to activate when we feel emotion. "Goosebumps really do happen in the brain," as Daniel Levitin said.[8]

Imagine the challenge for brain researchers in evaluating something ostensibly so subjective as the emotional effect of music. Until recently, the studies used only still images of brain activation. But music takes place over time, so how can we observe what's going on in the brain during the course of listening to a musical work? One method has been to look at the physiological effects over time. How, for example, does continued playing of a piece of music known to elicit a fear response change heart rate, electrodermal (skin) response, etc.?

Only recently have the emotional changes over time been observed through brain imaging. In Stefan Koelsch's fMRI study with regular/irregular chords, he looked at the physiological response to musical pieces over the length of the whole excerpt and also for different sections to measure changes in brain activity over time. He found that the reaction later in the excerpt was stronger, showing that the length of time we hear a musical piece affects the intensity of our response. Here again, music offers neuroscientists a unique opportunity to observe brain activity over time.[9]

Robert Zatorre at McGill University has gone a step further in studying the emotional effects of music over time. He and his student Valorie Salimpoor focused on the release of dopamine in the brain. Dopamine is the neurotransmitter believed to be responsible for indicating rewarding stimuli in our environment. It's what gets released when we eat certain food, take narcotic drugs, and enjoy sex, and it's released from the ventral part of the striatum in the brain. The striatum is part of the basal ganglia—a very old part of the brain in terms of human evolution. But Zatorre and Salimpoor saw a puzzle. Food and sex clearly have an evolutionary reward. And drugs have a reward that may feel more tangible than that of music. Certainly, we know experientially that listening to music and feeling our emotions aroused are linked. But the researchers wanted to *prove* that music creates a pleasure response in the brain—not just make a subjective judgment. And they wanted to look at the response to music over time. So they looked at brain activation fifteen seconds before the peak pleasure experience from a certain musical work (as rated by the subjects)—an effect that can be seen in the dorsal part of the striatum—and fifteen seconds after the peak experience, which can be observed in the ventral part of the striatum. The important finding is that they found *two parts* to the pleasure response: activity in both the

dorsal and ventral areas. The subjects were anticipating the pleasure response. And of course that makes perfect sense when we
think of the expectation/surprise factor when we react to music. Music theorists talk about tension building and then leading to a surprising harmonic shift—and then resolving back
to harmonic "home"—that expectation-surprise-expectation
cycle. Robert Zatorre says, with the thrill of scientific satisfac-
tion, that "we now think we have [identified] the biological
phenomenon behind that. The two parts to the pleasure response were never differentiated until now."[10]

Of course, each element of music helps shape our emotional
response. Pitch, rhythm, and tempo all play a role. Studies measuring Western subjects' responses to music confirm that fast-
tempo, Major-key music does indeed induce happiness as we
might expect it to, while slow, minor-key pieces invoke sadness.
Dissonant, rapid-tempo pieces produce fear and war chants
trigger adrenaline. Psychologist Carol Krumhansl did some of
the early studies on physiological and emotional responses to
music. Listeners were divided into three groups, one for each
piece of music. They moved a joystick for a computer screen to
indicate how much of a particular emotion they were feeling.
The "sad" excerpts, like Albinoni's Adagio, had slow tempos,
minor harmonies, and a fairly constant range of pitch and dynamics. The "fear" excerpts, like Mussorgsky's *Night on Bald
Mountain*, had rapid tempos, dissonant harmonies, and large
variations of dynamics and pitch. The "happy" excerpts, like
Vivaldi's "La Primavera" from *The Four Seasons,* had relatively
rapid tempos, dancelike rhythms, Major harmonies, and relatively constant ranges of pitch and dynamics. It should be noted

that these pieces were chosen for listeners attuned to Western tonality. There were big variations in emotions felt by listeners throughout each piece, though every person experienced peaks and valleys of emotion at the same moments in each piece.[11]

Brain imaging shows that several areas of the brain are involved in emotion, regions that are recently evolved as well as ones that humans developed very early on. For example, the amygdala and other limbic areas thought to have evolved very early in human development are associated with emotional responses and memories. It's been discovered that the amygdala may respond differently depending on whether the stimulus is positive or negative. And new studies indicate that one area of the amygdala may react to pleasant music and another to unpleasant music—as perceived by the listener. The amygdala plays a key role when the fight-or-flight response is triggered in our nervous system.

Recent data also shows that newer brain areas, such as the frontal cortex, are also triggered by emotional stimulation. It's fascinating that this particular area is activated by the temporal dynamic of music that creates experiences of expectation and surprise, tension and release.

There's so much research going on now regarding music and emotion that the area seems like a theme with countless variations. Neuroscientist Lawrence Parsons wondered if professional musicians feel the same emotions as listeners when they're performing. So he used a PET scanner to look at what's going on in their brains. The PET (positron emission tomography) shows blood flow to active parts of the brain. Parsons had pianists lie down in the scanner and play Bach's Italian Concerto, as well as scales, on a keyboard as their brains were being scanned. Surprisingly, it turned out that when they played Bach, the brain areas that would normally be emotionally involved were completely turned off. The areas for planning that are involved when we make decisions, like what to eat for dinner, were turned off as well. It's as though the performers' brains went into a kind of trance.[12]

Parsons asked rockers Jarvis Cocker and Richard Hawley if they experience something like that when they're performing. Cocker agreed that performance feels very different from listening:

> I mean you can just wallow in a song if you're at home. If it's something you really like. You know you can just lie there and . . . surrender yourself to it whereas . . . well, just the fact that you're actually singing it or performing it you know you've got to be kind of actively involved in it. The best performances, generally speaking, are the ones that I remember the least about; I've realized that. If you seem to have gone onstage and it all just goes—sssss—and then you're off the stage and an hour's passed but you're not really aware that an hour's passed, that usually means that it's been a good performance. Because somehow you've just done it. You've not gotten in the way of it. You've just allowed it to come out.[13]

Parsons's study indicates that performing musicians don't experience emotion in the same way as their audience.

Musicians talk of different kinds of "instinct" involved in performance as opposed to listening. Jarvis Cocker and Rich-

ard Hawley told me that when they're *listening* it's very clearly
an emotional response to the music.

> JARVIS COCKER: I mean, I do think that the initial "in" to
> music isn't an intellectual thing. You know, we're still in
> the brain here or whatever. But I think the initial re-
> sponse to a piece of music or a song is always instinctive
> and emotional. And you can analyze it later or what-
> ever, but whether you like something or not, you don't
> think about it.
>
> RICHARD HAWLEY: It's "yes or no" synapses. When I listen
> to it. I just go, "That's wrong or that's right."[14]

We all have an intuitive understanding of what we like and
how particular music manipulates our emotions. We *choose*
music—consciously and unconsciously to make us feel certain
ways in certain circumstances. John Sloboda and his colleagues at Keele University have been asking subjects to keep
diaries over a week's time. They're asked to make a note every
time they choose a particular piece of music. Then they fill out
a questionnaire: "Why did you want to play that piece? What
was your intention? Did you intend to change your mood? If
so, was it successful?" Sloboda also wants to know if people are
their own experts. Do they rely on other people's advice or are
they simply going with their own intuition? One subject had
made what she called a "chilled-out playlist"—consisting mostly
of drum and bass. She actually used it to calm herself down but
at the same time motivate herself while working when she had
a deadline. To some of us, that might seem a strange choice.
But for her it worked.[15]

Sloboda thinks that in this prepackaged age, people actually don't want someone else telling them what will make them feel good, or what will relax them and their babies. Certainly, those prepackaged soundtracks we hear all the time—in elevators, in stores to make us buy, in restaurants—are so annoying to many of us. Sloboda found that people are much more pleased with live music they hear in the street. After all, they can choose whether to stay and listen or walk away, just as we choose what concert to attend.[16]

Still, in today's world there are new ways of trying to choose music for us. There are Internet radio sites that hire "musicologists" who analyze songs, element by element, trying to identify qualities that appeal to certain listeners. And several companies are working on software to do the same thing. Music marketers of all sorts would certainly like to be able to predict what we like and what we'll buy.

But here's the thing that's very personal about our musical likes and dislikes. Yes, musical structure plays a big role in affecting our emotions. But so do our memories of particular pieces of music. We have cultural associations. And we also have very individual associations. There's the song we heard with our first boyfriend or girlfriend. Or in my case, the chamber music of a summer's night I heard in my childhood. Every time I hear one of those works today, those first experiences return. One study done about five years ago underlines how powerful musical memories can be. Patients with damage to brain structures known to be involved in both memory and emotion were able to recall music they knew and liked even though they had severe memory loss in other areas.

* * *

Separating memory from musical structure in terms of emotional impact is not a simple matter. In fact, the structure may actually contribute to our memory of the music. The brain maps out tonality in the prefrontal medial cortex—an area of the brain that also plays a key role in memory and in our sense of self. Petr Janata had a theory that there's an intimate relationship among emotions, music, and memory in that area that is also involved in our sense of self. For two years, he gathered data—and admits to being nervous about the results he'd find. Would he prove his hypothesis? He had thirteen UC Davis undergraduates listen to thirty-second fragments of songs that had been at the top of the pop and R&B charts during their childhood and teenage years. He put headphones on them and centered their heads under an fMRI scanner. For an hour, each student remained absolutely still—listening—while Janata ran the scans. The students indicated how pleasing or familiar each song was by tapping on a keyboard. They also indicated if they had any subjective memories of that song. Meanwhile, the fMRI scanner read the activations in their brains.[17]

Janata had to refine his methodology several times before he was able to pinpoint the exact brain activity at the exact time each student heard a song. And sure enough, the data proved Janata's theory. Some of his brain images described in chapter 2 (see page 9 in the color insert) actually show how music moves in tonal space.

Janata thinks he's on the verge of an even more important discovery. He believes the experience of memory—and emotion—is "embedded within how our brains work. Music engages basic brain circuitry that's in place for our survival and well-being. But it engages it in a way that's pleasurable for us. If the brain is actively seeking out musical engagement, we can turn that around and ask why the brain seeks music, and that way answer a fundamental question about the neuroscience of the brain."

Neuroscientist Larry Parsons has found evidence that unexpected brain areas are also activated when we have a highly pleasurable music-listening experience associated with a powerful memory. Parsons did fMRI scans with a subject listening to various music selections that he himself selected as being pleasurable (see the color insert). There was a very dramatic—and unexpected—result when the subject chose one of Richard Strauss's *Four Last Songs* sung by a soprano he knew as a friend. What surprised Parsons was that there was really widespread activity all over the brain for this particular piece sung by the subject's friend, somebody he knew. "This music meant something to him," Parsons says.[18]

Music may even appeal to primal human memories. Larry Parsons has found another remarkable aspect of how emotion registers in the brain when we listen to music, to song—human and otherwise! Parsons analyzed brain areas activated when subjects listen to human song and to birdsong. He picked songs unfamiliar to the subjects this time. And he teamed up with a bird biologist to select samples of birdsong. One subject was a birdsong expert, one was a musician who didn't listen to birdsong, and the third was neither a music expert nor a bird expert. Parsons himself was surprised to see that the scans showed the listeners showed *more* emotion when they heard birdsong as compared to listening to beautiful songs sung by a human voice. There was a wider range of response listening to birdsong, with more activity in the emotion areas, executive planning areas, and auditory areas of the brain.[19]

Parsons plans to do more extensive studies. One possible explanation for the increased brain activity when subjects listened to birdsong is that they were trying to find the patterns in the birdsong; human song is more familiar. But Parsons also thinks this early result may have important implications for our understanding of the role music played in human evolution. Perhaps early *Homo sapiens* found pleasure in birdsong and was inspired to imitate it with human music. The role of music in human evolution is a topic we'll explore further in chapter 8.

The study of musical emotion is still in its infancy. Fifteen years ago, scientists dismissed the idea of trying to study the subject at all. They thought it impossible to apply rigorous scientific methods to a topic thought to be so subjective, so mysterious, even mystical. But today, neuroscientists around the world are busy trying to map musical emotion in the brain. There is recognition that music's effect on the body, the brain, and our emotions cannot be separated. Music is central to our physiology, our psychology, and our very identity and sense of self. It makes us forget our fear and stress. It awakens our oldest memories.

⟆ CHAPTER 6 ⟅

Mind-Bending Notes:
Can Music Make Us Smarter?

Music can change the world because it can change people.

—BONO, U2

ⓨ

A little girl is focusing with utter concentration; she's playing the cello, reading the music, coordinating her left
hand on the fingerboard and her bow arm. She's playing
well. The question is: What's happening in her brain? Is music
changing it?

This young musician happens to be the daughter of one of
the leading scientists trying to answer that question. Dr. Gottfried Schlaug is a neurologist and director of the Music and
Neuroimaging Laboratory at Boston's Beth Israel Deaconess
Hospital and Harvard Medical School. He's a trained organist
himself. He's always had a passion for music; now he wants to
know if music training can actually affect our brain and cogni-

tive development.[1] It's a field of research that for three decades has been fraught with rumor and media hype. Can music improve mathematical abilities? Can playing music to your child or infant—or even to the fetus—make a difference? Schlaug is among numerous researchers doing studies that have brought new evidence and insight to the subject.

It's thrilling to learn that the brains of musicians are actually physically different from those of nonmusicians. Schlaug and others, including neuroscientist Robert Zatorre, have found that some areas of the cortex, the outer surface of the brain that contains "gray matter" or the nerve cells called neurons, are thicker in people with musical training and that motor and auditory regions also have more connections. The areas that show the greatest change and reveal the most consistent findings across different laboratories are in the auditory part of the brain (responsible for discriminating sounds and sound memories) and the motor part of the brain, which is responsible for coordinated, conscious movement. Zatorre points out that we don't yet know how this occurs. He asks, "Does that mean that there are more cells there? Does it mean the cells are organized differently? Does it mean that the connections in between the cells are different somehow? Before we did this kind of research we didn't even know to ask these questions."[2]

A team of researchers found that the auditory cortex contains *130 percent* more gray matter in professional musicians than in nonmusicians. This study also found that the professionals have 102 percent more activity in their auditory cortex than nonmusicians. Amateur musicians had 37 percent more activity in their brains on average than those who did not play an instrument—impressive figures.[3] However, this study has not been replicated.

One intriguing aspect is that areas of the frontal cortex are also different in musicians. And that's the region, Zatorre explains, "that does some of the most complicated and interesting things in human cognition. It does planning and higher order thinking; and it does language." Zatorre found that the frontal regions have dense connections with auditory regions and frontal regions are important in linking sounds with motor actions, either hand actions or articulatory actions. He also discovered another brain area that's different in musicians— the corpus callosum, which links the two sides of the brain. And he found that it's particularly enlarged in the brains of instrumentalists who started musical training early.[4] In a longitudinal— long-term—study comparing children who learned to play musical instruments to those that did not, the corpus callosum and the motor regions showed changes in the instrumental group that were not seen in the noninstrumental group. This result provides a reason, or "causality," Schlaug says, for the between-group differences seen in previous studies. The corpus callosum communicates between the two brain hemispheres. And it lets both sides of the brain coordinate movements—say, left and right hands.

It's possible that self-selection could play a role. That is, the question arises whether people who decide to start intensive musical training *already* had larger corpus callosums that might enable them to play an instrument more easily. But Schlaug discounts the possibility that such structural disparities are inborn in people who become professional musicians. He and other scientists are quite convinced and have recently found clear evidence in longitudinal studies that musical training does create new or enhanced connections in some parts of the brain.[5]

This research with trained musicians is part of a huge shift in our understanding of the brain itself that has occurred recently. Scientists used to think our brains are more or less fixed once we reach adulthood. But one of the hottest topics today in neuroscience is neuroplasticity: We now know that our brains change; they continue "learning" even in adulthood. New experiences create new networks of neurons that communicate with each other. And experiences similar to ones we already know actually reinforce already established neural networks.

In a way, examples of neuroplasticity have been right before our eyes and ears in the musical world. Consider famous blind musicians like Stevie Wonder, Ray Charles, and Andrea Bocelli. It seems amazing that they're able to perform at such a high level without sight. But it's probably *because* of their blindness, not in spite of it. Robert Zatorre believes that these musicians are able to call on parts of the brain that ordinarily would be handling vision to contribute to their ability to create music. These brain areas get co-opted to do auditory processing and help out in enhancing musical abilities. Blind people often develop more sensitive ears, with better than average hearing, according to Zatorre's studies. He showed me brain scans comparing activity in the visual area of the cortex in sighted people and blind people. It was no surprise that sighted people show no activity in the visual area of the cortex when they're hearing sound. But in blind subjects, one clearly sees the visual part of the brain responding.[6]

Larry Parsons decided to do a fun experiment with a friend of his—British archaeologist Steven Mithen. Mithen is an avid music listener and also writes about its role in human history. But he'd never studied music or tried to play or sing. In fact, he was a terrible singer, not able to hold a tune at all. So Parsons persuaded him to take singing lessons for a year. Parsons scanned Mithen's brain before and after the lessons to see if there were any changes. And there were. Several brain areas showed increased activity after a year of singing lessons. The area that showed the strongest increased activity was in the temporal lobe (involved in auditory processing) and the superior plenum parietal region. It's an area Parsons and others have shown to be active for representing musical structure. So the conclusion is that Mithen's brain had developed new connections or neural networks to process music. Mithen still didn't sing too well, though he was better. And he says, "I was astonished that just within a year I could have manipulated my brain in that way."[7]

Robert Zatorre is looking to future applications for these findings regarding music and brain plasticity. "We need to understand the how and why of these effects," he says. "Because if we can figure out how one part of the brain is able to stand in for another part, well, the implications of that are enormous."[8] Perhaps one part of the brain can be trained intentionally and precisely to take over for another part.

And if music can change the brains of adults in such dramatic ways, how might it affect the development of children's brains? Specifically, can music make a child smarter?

If music can physically change the brain, the intuitive answer to that question is yes. But it's not so simple to really prove scientifically. When research on the topic began to explode a couple of decades ago, early results were exciting but proved problematic. In 1993, researchers Gordon Shaw of the University of California, Irvine, and Frances Rauscher at the University of Wisconsin, Oshkosh, published the results of research indicating that listening to Mozart's Sonata K. 448 for two pianos seemed to boost student scores on a test of visualization tasks related to spatial reasoning.[9] The report of this result spawned a marketing frenzy as entrepreneurs moved to cash in. And the governor of Georgia suggested a budget to give every child born in the state a CD of classical music.

Some musicians and music lovers were pleased by the attention but disturbed that it was maybe for the wrong reasons. After all, music should be valued for its own sake, not just because it might improve children's grades in other areas. Many in the science world were troubled because other researchers were not able to consistently replicate the Rauscher-Shaw results. And when these follow-up studies did show some improvement in nonmusic skills it proved to be short-lived. The change in performance didn't hold up over time.

The controversy as to whether just *listening* to certain music—in the womb or after birth—can improve intelligence did drive scientists around the world to start new studies aimed at answering that question: Can music make my child smarter? With the evidence that listening alone seemed to bring short-term results, if any, researchers began to focus on creating and performing music. Would learning to play an instrument or to sing produce positive effects in behavioral and cognitive domains related—or even not related—to the domains being trained by practicing an instrument? Gottfried Schlaug is one of the pioneer investigators. It's not surprising that music training brings changes in brain areas directly related to music performance—auditory and motor regions. But the big debate has been about whether music training really can lead to improved abilities in other areas such as language, vocabulary, visual or spatial skills, and math. And only longitudinal studies conducted over time can provide solid answers.

Schlaug and his colleague Ellen Winner designed two studies with children just starting lessons to learn a musical instrument. They were matched to a control group from the same neighborhood made up of children who were not taking music lessons. After sixteen months, the instrument-training group did show improvement in the skills directly associated with music—fine motor skills and auditory discrimination skills. Similarly, changes were seen in motor and auditory regions of the brains in the instrument-training children that were not seen in the other group. Some of the biggest changes were in the corpus callosum. But after sixteen months, there seemed to be no change in the skills not so directly related to music. This suggests that longer observation periods or more intense training may be required for these cognitive effects to appear. Schlaug and Winner are, of course, continuing the study and following the children with a final assessment after four years of instrumental training.

To more quickly gather data about the long-term effects of music training, Schlaug organized a second study with children around ten years of age who'd already had three to six years of musical training. These children also showed clear differences when they were compared to a matched group of children without instrument training. But they also showed differences in what Schlaug calls the "far-transfer domains" including vocabulary skills and visual reasoning ability. The subjects were asked to do various visual puzzle exercises like the ones where one has to figure out what image fits with others in a series. Schlaug says he was initially puzzled as to why music training would have this last effect. What does music have to do with our ability to make sense of what we see? But he concluded that musicians actually use a lot of visual reasoning skills in reading music, which actually is deciphering single symbols, combinations, and patterns of symbols and translating them into motor commands. And even when they're not reading music, musicians also use visual pattern memory and the matching of patterns. Schlaug did not find in this study that other visual spatial skills were enhanced.[10] This study in nine- to eleven-year-old children was a cross-sectional comparison of an instrumental group with a noninstrumental group. These comparisons can reveal trends and correlations. But by themselves they're still enough to establish clear proof that instrumental music training causes brain and cognitive differences.

Schlaug's chief interest is in what music making does to the brain. But he realizes that studies like his have major implications for education. He says:

> It's certainly possible that through music particular topics could be taught in a different way. It's also possible that music itself primes regions in the brain, or opens up different channels, to processing that we might not get with traditional ways of teaching. I don't think it's a one-to-one relationship that the more music you play to your child or the

more music a child plays the smarter this child will become. But I think there is something to the idea that engaging in music making has beneficial effects on brain development and cognitive skills.[11]

He thinks the reason for this probably has to do with the fact that playing or singing music engages many areas of the brain. Some of these areas might also be used for other functions. It is this "cross-talk," Schlaug says, that might be underlying some of the cognitive enhancements that people have described in music-making experiments. That brain orchestra in our heads is activating and, most likely, building neural networks.[12]

The irony is that while school music education programs continue to be cut, there remains great interest in the potential of music education among consumers. And many who believe in the benefits of musical training and exposure want to start early. There are several devices on the market today designed to convey music even to the fetus in the womb. Some pregnant mothers are strapping them to their bellies so that their un-born children will be exposed to the sound of classical music.[13]

It's true that starting at around eighteen weeks, fetuses can hear. They listen to the mother's heartbeat, voices, and other noises around them. So why not let them hear "good music"? One study in the *Journal of Child Development* also showed that fetuses, starting at thirty weeks, can acclimate to sounds over time and they develop memory at three to four weeks.[14] But this whole field of prenatal music listening remains a matter of debate.

Some school systems are gathering evidence to support the argument for early music training. In Alpine, Colorado, the school district started a program that teaches kindergartners through third graders math and music. Teachers say they've seen improvement in the kids' academic performance since the program began.[15] In Baltimore, researcher Barbara Helmrich at the College of Notre Dame did a study looking at the algebra scores of ninth graders in six Maryland school districts. She divided the students into three groups: those who had formal training on a musical instrument during the sixth, seventh, and eighth grades; those who received choral instruction during those same years; and those who received no formal musical training. And she found that the children who had studied music outperformed the other group in a significant way. The best algebra scores were earned by the musical instrument group. The next best scores were earned by the choral group. Helmrich noted that the gap in achievement was largest among African American students. That means that "offering music education in middle school might present an alternative strategy for narrowing the achievement gap," Helmrich wrote.[16]

Since math is built into the foundations of sound and music, many people think it's a proven fact that if one is good at math, one is good at music—and vice versa. Actually, there's no hard proof of that. But results like those from the Maryland algebra study are beginning to add fact to intuition.

There's more research now showing a link between music training and language ability. One very interesting study took place in Leipzig, Germany, home of the world-famous St. Thomas Boys Choir. Sebastian Jentschke, a young scientist at the Max Planck Institute, thought the choirboys would be ideal subjects for a study since they receive such intensive music training. It's fitting that this important study was done in

Leipzig, home to that city's Max Planck Institute and to so many great composers—a true marriage of art and science. The institute itself embodies the union of science and art. It's part of the Max Planck Society for the Advancement of Science, a publicly funded German organization. Its eighty institutes conduct basic research in various scientific fields as well as in the arts and humanities.

Jentschke, who's passionate about classical music, also saw the synchronicity in doing this study in Leipzig—a place where science and music come together. The spun-gold voices of the choir fill St. Thomas Church where Bach was the choirmaster. And the city was also the home of Mendelssohn and Schumann. Wagner was born there. Walk the streets in Leipzig and one feels classical music all around.[17]

The idea behind Jentschke's study was to investigate syntax processing in music and in language. Both music and language are organized from simple elements like phonemes (sounds) and tones. These elements are combined through complex sequences that are structured according to certain patterns. Those regular patterns are called syntax. In language, syntax is grammar. Music has its own syntax in the combination of intervals and chords. When Jentschke began his study a few years ago, there was evidence that musical syntax and linguistic syntax are processed in comparable regions of the human brain. But the question was whether one could prove a clear effect between musical training and improved ability to process linguistic syntax.

I visited Jentschke's lab to see how he conducted the experiment. He demonstrated with one of the choirboys who'd participated in the study. The scene was rather surreal. The little boy was fitted with a red cap covered with electrodes that would measure the EEG or electrical activity in his brain.

The boy sat in a chair with headphones, listening to different linguistic and musical sequences. The experiment actually had two parts—one for music and one for language. For the music part, different sets of chords were played for the subjects. The chord sequences either ended on a regular, expected tone according to the Western musical system, or on a less-expected chord that violated what a person would expect when listening. The difference between the chord sequences was fairly subtle. A musically trained ear would react more strongly to the irregular chords.

In the language experiment, the subjects listened to syntactically correct and incorrect sentences. For example an incorrect sentence might be "the cat was in caught the garden" while the correct version would be "the cat was caught in the garden."

Jentschke compared the EEG responses in the language test of the children with musical training to those with no music training. And he found that the choirboys—those with musical training—performed much better on processing linguistic syntax. That is, their brains reacted more strongly to the incorrect sentences. Their brains used a larger number of neurons for this task. Jentschke was very excited about the result, which was pioneering.[18]

Also, this finding about the cross-pollination between music and language skills could be used to help children who are delayed in their language development, and perhaps even help those with language-processing differences and disabilities. Jentschke's lab also did a study to find out if children with what's called a specific language impairment, who have problems processing grammar, also have trouble processing musical syntax. The answer was yes. So probably these children could be trained using music to improve their language skills.[19]

Again, Sebastian Jentschke felt the result carried significance beyond the science itself. "I like it very much especially because it has implication for education. It shows that it is important to learn a musical instrument or to sing because it can train processes in other cognitive domains."[20]

Leading music/science researchers now agree there's no question that music training has repercussions on brain anatomy. As neuroscientist Robert Zatorre points out, "This in itself until a few years ago, no one had an inkling that this was going on."[21]

No doubt other kinds of training also impact brain anatomy. And there's more work to be done to identify all the specific effects of music training. But it's clear that this exciting line of inquiry is going to provide hard scientific evidence that educators should consider.

Many musicians certainly believe that early musical training is extremely important. Haitian American violinist and composer Daniel Bernard Roumain (DBR) grew up in Florida and started playing in public school. "Sometimes instruments choose you," he told me. "I feel that the violin just called out my name." One day he was walking past a classroom in Margate Elementary School and the door was open. He heard kids playing the violin. "I'd never heard anything like that before. I had never seen an orchestra. I don't think I really knew what a violin was. And I was completely hypnotized by it, captivated by it." A few days later, he walked into that classroom and told the teacher he wanted to learn to play the violin. He became the first Margate kindergartner to take violin lessons. "You know, it's sad," DBR continued, "because that was over thirty years ago and I have a very strong feeling I may be the last Margate Stringer. Because in the public school system in Broward Country, if you want to play the violin now, in some cases you have to wait until high school. Those instruments, my teacher are all gone."[22]

That story is being repeated all over America—music classes sacrificed to budget cuts.

"You know, it's a sobering thought," DBR said, "because if not for the violin, my life would have been very different. Music not only changed my life. I feel it saved my life. So of course the question is, how many lives are being lost now, you know? Well, there's action to be taken."[23]

DBR has taken action. He helped start the Florida Youth Orchestra. And he has also worked with New York City public schoolchildren in conjunction with the Orchestra of St. Luke's Young Composers Program. The program teaches kids as young as seven to compose—even if they've never played music, never even learned to *read* music. The techniques involve hands-on learning and imagination. DBR points out that "music notation is by its very nature graphic notation. It's just a bunch of symbols. Lines and dots and circles on a piece of paper." So using that idea, the Young Composers Program uses different kinds of symbols. The children can cut out a picture from a magazine and ask a musician to play a certain sound every time they see that image. Then they put images together as a collage. And there's a musical composition. They also use numerical music—a method in which numbers are assigned a note. So

1-1-2-1-2-3-1-2-3-4 becomes a tune and a rhythm. Try it, just reading the numbers to yourself.

Sometimes the children in the Young Composers Program tell a story with music. They take a character and decide that a flute, for example, suits that character. They assign different instruments to other characters. Then there's an exchange between the characters. DBR explains, "It's a way for them to think of music in nonmusical terms."[24] Many of the children in the program go on to play instruments and to compose real works that the Orchestra of St. Luke's musicians perform.

Maestro Daniel Barenboim, the renowned pianist and conductor, is also a passionate advocate for early music education and exposure. He's founded Musikkindergartens in the Middle East and in Berlin. Barenboim's idea is to immerse children in music and integrate it with every other aspect of their school day. He explains:

> The Musikkindergarten is not a kindergarten for little musicians; it is not a musical education but education through music. The children receive assistance from their teachers and from members of the Staatskapelle Berlin [the symphony orchestra] in their contact with music, with the different sounds that exist in music; they are allowed to discover what kind of story music can tell them. Through their musical experiences they learn all the things that children normally learn in kindergarten: discipline, playfulness, affection, and so on. They learn these things with and through the music. Visiting the kindergarten makes me wish I could be three years old again![25]

The children actually play with music. Yes, they play—on the piano, drums, and other instruments. But they treat music *as* play. Two little girls sat at the piano improvising a melody. One had her stuffed animal play some notes on the keyboard. They danced to music. They went to sleep and woke up to music. "This naturalness of contact with music and with the act of listening to and making music, this is what I want the kids to have," Barenboim says.

The director of the Berlin Musikkindergarten, Stephanie Uibel, says they have evidence that their children, especially those who started at a low level of social competence, improve their social networking skills after one or two years in the school. After all, doing music together is a very social activity. Also, the language abilities of the Musikkindergarten kids are higher compared to children in regular kindergartens.[26]

The hope is that the Musikkindergarten model will spread through Germany, the Middle East, and other parts of the world.

CHAPTER 7

Music Speaks

Music is the universal language of mankind.

—LONGFELLOW

When I attend a chamber music or jazz concert, I can feel the musicians talking to each other in the language of their art. For them, music *is* a language. It is for us, too, in the sense that it affects and changes us. But what exactly is the relationship between music and verbal language? Is music really as much of a human "voice" as the words we use to communicate? Clearly, recent neuroscience is showing that there is some sort of relationship between language and music. But when it comes to how our abilities for song and speech function in the brain, there are still mysteries to be explored.

Some evidence suggests that there are distinct areas in the brain for speech and for music: A person who loses speech may retain the ability to perceive and process music, and vice versa. Stroke patients are the classic example. The early research into the relationship between music and language focused on such patients who had deficits in either language or music due to some kind of brain lesion. Either they had a neurologic disorder such as a stroke or they had brain damage because of an accident. Some patients have lost the ability to speak, but not their musical ability. This is the condition called aphasia. One stroke patient could not form words at all, but when the researcher played "Happy Birthday" to him, he could easily sing along. This particular man had never had music lessons, but there are also stories of famous composers, like Sebalin, who suffered strokes but retained their musical abilities. Isabelle Peretz, a psychologist at McGill University in Montreal, was one of the pioneer scientists who studied these patients.

She has also studied subjects who are amusic—that is, they can speak perfectly well but have no musical abilities. They do not have normal pitch perception. If one plays "Happy Birthday" to them without the words, they cannot identify the song. Peretz strongly believes that these cases argue that music and language abilities are separated in the brain.

The current estimate is that about 4 percent of the general population are amusics. That's actually very small considering that so many people think they have no musical ability and can't carry a tune. As we remember from pitch-perception experiments by scientists like Daniel Levitin, most of us actually *can* perceive pitch quite accurately.[1] Peretz believes that amusics, who typically do not have difficulties with speaking or listening, provide more evidence that music and language use separate networks or processes in the brain. She acknowledges that some components of the two systems may be shared but stands by her conviction that fundamentally they are distinct.

There are scientists who see a more complex picture regarding the relationship between music and language processing in the brain. Larry Parsons did a brain-scanning study comparing music and language directly in the same subjects. This study was the first to look at musical improvisation and the brain. In life, we make up sentences and phrases all the time when we speak. So, Parsons wondered, is that ability comparable in terms of what's going on in the brain when we improvise music? His subjects were given parts of sentences and parts of melodies. Then they were asked to complete them while carrying on the meaning of the sentence or melody. That is, they had to complete a sentence so it made sense and complete a melody fragment to make musical sense within the key and rhythm that had been established. What Parsons found was that there are a set of brain activities common to the creation of both language and music.[2]

Some of these common areas would be expected. Auditory and motor areas were activated when people finished a sentence or a melody that they sang. But then Parsons found more areas that were activated when generating a melody. Some were regions related to planning while some were auditory areas—probably specialized for melodic and harmonic structure. But Parsons was surprised by the other areas that were activated. One was on the left, adjacent to Broca's area, which is known to be involved with language processing. And there was another in the same region as Broca's but on the right. These two regions, Parsons says, are probably involved in planning the construction of organized melodic phrases. And the right area is one known to be involved in dance. No one had ever before identified these areas as being associated with composing melodies, and no one had shown that music is so closely related to language and to dance in the brain. So music, language, and dance may all be connected as forms of communication.[3]

Parsons says, "This particular study suggests that music and language systems are not completely distinct brain systems. There are components of music and components of language that appear to be distinct and other components that appear to be shared and then some components which lie adjacent to each other."[4]

When British rock singer Jarvis Cocker met Parsons, he was very eager to ask about the relationship between music and language. Cocker, who's also a songwriter, says he never reads the music and lyrics together before he performs because the words and notes seem totally disconnected. When he looks at the page, he explains, the two don't seem to work as a song. So, Cocker wondered, perhaps music and language really are separated somehow in the brain. But Parsons explained that *written music* is a different matter altogether. Yes, reading words while we imagine hearing something is a strange thing for our brain because the brain is set up for *speaking and hearing* language and *making and hearing* music—not putting words and notes down on paper. Writing is a skill that human beings evolved much later, probably six thousand years ago. Music is thought to have developed maybe five hundred thousand years ago. Early man responded to the sound, the vibration of music and words around the campfire, singing and dancing.[5]

Parsons's and other neuroscientists' work seems to fit with another experiment, done from a different perspective, by Ani

Patel, neurobiologist at The Neurosciences Institute in San Diego. Patel has focused much of his research on the music/language connection. He was intrigued by the apparent similarity between the sound of music and spoken language in countries around the world. He played two samples of music for me and asked me to guess which was by an English composer and which was by a French composer. Like most listeners, I was able—without knowing the music or names of the composers—to identify them correctly. One was by Edward Elgar, an English composer, and one was by Claude Debussy, who was French. And both segments did sound distinctly English and French respectively. But Patel did a more scientific analysis. Using a computer, he compared rhythms and patterns of music to those of everyday spoken language in English and French. He measured the length of notes in the music and the length of vowels in spoken sentences of English and French. And he found that in English, longer vowels alternate more often with shorter vowels than is the case in French. French has a more languorous rhythm than English. Patel says, "What's happening is that when we learn our native language part of what we learn is the timing and the rhythm. And we extract that as listeners and composers do, too."

Patel believes that "we recruit parts of the language system when we process music and we incorporate it into the wonderful set of brain networks that we use to understand music and make sense of music." He theorizes that the processing of rhythm is similar in both music and speech."[6]

Sebastian Jentschke's study showed how linguistic syntax processing improves with music training.[7] And Patel believes that there is an overlap in the cognitive processing of language

and music—that music and language syntax share neural networks. He argues that despite their many obvious differences
in form and function, music and language share deep neural
connections.[8]

This overlap between neural networks may start very early.
Kathleen Wermke, the German researcher who did the fascinating analysis finding musical intervals in the cries of infants,[9]
also looked into perception of melody and language in the
womb and right after birth. With colleagues at the Center for
Prespeech Development at the University of Würzburg,
Wermke analyzed the crying patterns of thirty French and
thirty German newborns. They were looking for melody and
intensity contours in the cries. The French newborns produced
rising melody shapes while the German infants more often
produced falling shapes. Now what does this mean? We know
now that the fetus starts auditory learning in the third trimes-
ter of gestation. And what is the fetus listening to? The mother's
voice—and other voices in the native language—that penetrate
the mother's belly, albeit in a muffled way. So the newborn has
actually memorized the contours of the mother's native language. And the intonation patterns of spoken French and German correspond to the cries of the infant subjects. French is
characterized by a rise in pitch right toward the end of words
and phrases. German typically has a falling melody contour.
Other researchers had already found that French infants have
more rising melody contours than English and Japanese infants.
And it's also been shown that at four months of age French and
German toddlers had language-specific references for stress
patterns. But the excitement about Wermke's recent study
was that it shows an even earlier relationship to the native

language—a relationship that must have begun even before birth.

Sandra Trehub, who specializes in studying infant response to musical intervals at her Toronto lab, points to "motherese"— the way mothers vocalize to their babies—as a great example of the link between music and language. "Motherese" is that kind of singsong musical speech that communicates emotion to babies and can put them into a trancelike state, and it exists across cultures.[10]

One of the most thought-provoking theories about the relationship between music and language was developed at Duke University by David Schwartz, Catherine Howe, and Dale Purves. They propose that we look to language—not just to math—to find the very foundation of music.[11] There's no question that there *is* a physics of sound based on the frequencies of vibration. And there are relationships between those frequencies: intervals. As noted earlier, people around the world all seem to find certain intervals pleasurable, particularly the octave and to some degree the fifth and fourth. The link between these simple ratios and harmony has driven music theory for centuries. Neuroscientists theorize that the brain actually is wired to respond to those intervals. So the thinking is that biology has adapted to the physics of sound.

The Duke researchers believe that biology may in fact be the leader in terms of our natural response to those intervals. They don't think that music is simply a mathematical abstraction, somehow separate from the natural world around us. They feel there must be some explanation for the fact that listeners over time and across the world respond the same way to the octave, fifth, and fourth. And in virtually all cultures, musical sound is divided into some or all of the twelve intervals of semitones within an octave that make up the chromatic scale. The Duke scientists thought the answer must lie with our auditory system. And they were surprised that even with the recent explosion in neuroscience research, there was still no proven explanation either in physiological or psychological terms.

So the Duke team reasoned that our perception of tone is likely shaped by the sounds around us. There are many variables in the sound information our brains must process. Probably, the Duke scientists reasoned, the brain learns to predict the likelihood of certain sounds to which it will respond. And what more common sound is there than our own speech? They decided to analyze frequencies in speech and compare them to the frequency combinations in music that we find pleasant or harmonious. They took more than one hundred thousand segments of speech from a variety of languages from all over the world. They didn't care about sentences or meaning—just pure sound. They made note of which frequencies were most commonly emphasized in speech, and found that the set of frequencies with the most emphasis in all languages corresponded almost exactly to the chromatic scale, those twelve intervals within an octave.[12] David Schwartz says, "Music, like the visual arts, is rooted in our experience of the natural world. It emulates our sound environment in the way that visual arts emulate the visual environment." This theory argues that with music we are singing the song of ourselves.

What came first, music or language? This question has become a very hot topic in music/science research. In fact it's surrounded by more emotion than any other subject in the field. The debate began with a comment made by renowned Harvard cognitive psychologist and linguist Steven Pinker. In his 1997 book *How the Mind Works*,[13] Pinker wrote that music is "auditory cheesecake"—a pleasurable offshoot of our linguistic ability and not anything essential to human survival in an evolutionary sense. More recently, Pinker explained further what he meant:

> I think many people, including many scientists, want music to be an adaptation because they feel that that would ratify its value in human life. It would ennoble it, make it part of our nature. But I think we should resist that. It may indeed be part of our nature. But it may not necessarily be an adaptation in the biologist's sense. Unlike other traits—fear of heights, language, sexual desire, where it's fairly straightforward to see how it would've enhanced reproduction and survival, music is not so obvious.[14]

Pinker went on to say that there's no question how important language is to convey information—information that may be crucial to survival. He says, "You can't tell a story with music unless you already know what the story is. A simple plot like boy meets girl, there's no way you could play a sequence of notes and have the person listening to them know that that's what you had in mind."[15]

Moreover, Pinker questions the value of the degree of emotion music can convey. He asks why it's so good to feel sad when "no one has died or to feel excited when there's nothing to feel excited about."[16]

Musicians and music lovers certainly would argue that music does tell stories—in its own terms—and that the value of music's emotional impact is perhaps immeasurable in subjective terms, yet *can* be measured in physical and psychological terms.

Yet evolutionary biology does dictate that for a behavioral or cognitive capacity to be innate to our species, it would have to confer on us some advantage for adapting, surviving, and reproducing, like helping mothers calm babies, attracting the opposite sex, and helping build community. And there are leading figures in the music/science field who agree with Pinker that music may well have been a later human invention, not an evolutionary adaptation like language. Neuroscientist Robert Zatorre is one. He thinks music may well be the consequence of several other adaptations. There were selective pressures, for example, to evolve acute hearing abilities, or to move our fingers very precisely because those skills helped us survive. But perhaps there wasn't selective pressure for music itself.[17] The late famous paleontologist Stephen Jay Gould also regarded music and the other arts as mere spin-offs developed in an oversize human brain—of no interest to evolutionary science. Ani Patel finds the whole argument about which came first, music or language, a false one. He doesn't think we need to choose between deciding that music is innate or that it's some trivial, pleasurable, late-developing frill that we can easily live without. He believes music is a human invention like written language. Language was probably an evolutionary adaptation. But writing was not. Still, writing has transformed human life. Patel maintains that "music is something that we invented a long time ago from the resources that we have in our brain, from the many different cognitive systems that evolution did shape us to have. It absolutely transformed our emotional lives. It transformed our ability to store memories. And it changes the structure of our brain."

Patel thinks all this happened early on in human evolution. He likens the invention of music to the invention of a transformative technology. "Music is like our inner fire that we created and that we'll never live without."[18]

Physics and math and biology all seem to be involved in the discussion regarding the true roots or origins of music. No matter which may ultimately be shown to take precedence, it's notable that all these ways of understanding our natural world and our existence in it are connected to music. But science is eager for more evidence. And one doesn't have to look far in the music/science field to find adamant opponents to Pinker's theory. There are many.

One scientist who has plunged deeply into the debate is Steven Mithen, the British archaeologist. Mithen believes Pinker "got something deeply wrong. How can we respond so emotionally and so intuitively to music," Mithen asks, "if it isn't something that's really deeply embedded in our biology? How can that be?"[19]

꞊ CHAPTER 8 ꞊

Why Music?

Music is too precise to express in words.

—FELIX MENDELSSOHN

☙

On a hillside in Southern Germany, some thirty-five thousand years ago, the sounds of a flute wafted in the breeze. Our ancestors—Stone Age human beings—lived in the cave cut into the hill. They gazed out over the valley and made music.

In 2008, I traveled to this region, accompanied by archaeologists Steven Mithen and Nicholas Conard, an American who works in Germany at the University of Tübingen. Conard and his team have discovered the earliest-known musical instruments— ancient flutes carved from the bones of swans and the ivory tusks of mammoths. Mithen had heard about the discoveries, but had never seen these early examples of music-making tools.

Mithen has spent his career studying human evolution and looking for what makes humans different from all other species of animals. He has looked at factors such as how we walk and how we talk and how we think. But Mithen acknowledges that for years he neglected music, even though he himself often writes to music. Bach is a particular favorite. And he told me he had a kind of epiphany—sparked in part by Pinker's book *How the Mind Works*. He began to think, he said, that "through music I can engage with my evolutionary past almost as much as I could by looking at fossils and stone artifacts. When I began this line of research I thought music was important," he continued. "I've realized that it's even vastly more important than I imagined."[1]

So Mithen decided to use his experience and skills as an archaeologist to investigate the roots of music in human history—and even prehuman history. The question that drove him as it's driving other music scientists is "Why music?" Why did humans develop music in the first place? What purpose, if any, does it serve?[2] To explore the answer, we must go back in time to the Neanderthals and then look to other animals' experience of music and music-like communication for further clues about the evolution of music.

At the time of our visit, in the spring of 2008, Nicholas Conard and his archaeologist colleagues from Tübingen had found fragments of flutes carved from the bones of swans here at the Hohle Fels cave west of Ulm. These flutes were thought to be around thirty-five thousand years old, though the dating was imprecise. Then, shortly after that find, Conard and his colleagues found an even older flute nearby in a cave at Geissenklösterle. This one had four finger holes and was carved from the ivory tusk of a mammoth. The archaeologists had to piece it together from thirty-one tiny fragments. But one can clearly see the mouth end and the distal end. This is an artifact, a piece of history. But it seems alive, ready to make music again.[3]

In the spring of 2009, Conard announced that he'd found another flute, one with five finger holes (see the color insert), at Hohle Fels—this one even more ancient than the Geissen-klösterle specimen. And this time, the archaeologists were able to date it more precisely, to at least thirty-five thousand years old, perhaps forty thousand. These flutes provide compelling evidence that human beings of the Stone Age had a musical culture.[4]

Nicholas Conard says that with this five-finger-hole flute, made out of a griffin vulture radius, one can play any song you can hum. Experts who have examined it say it is actually more technologically advanced than modern instruments. It has a forked mouthpiece, which allows the player to put a cut in the air column. And the first finger hole may have a cut in the air column as well. This produces a range of notes "with enormous possibilities for musical experience," Conard explains. For Co-nard, this remarkable ancient flute means that "we're dealing with a very sophisticated musical tradition at a very early age."[5]

Before Conard's discoveries, the earliest sure evidence of musical instruments came from France and Austria, but these specimens were dated much more recently—less than thirty thousand years ago. Conard, Mithen, and other archaeologists see these amazing flutes as a strong indication that music is and has been an integral part of human existence. Here in these German caves, found among bones of bears and mam-moths and chips of stone from a toolmaking shop, the flutes prove that these people who were struggling simply to survive still had a musical, artistic life. The fact that the flutes were found lying among the remnants of daily life suggests that music *was* a part of daily life.

Copies of the first Hohle Fels and Geissenklösterle flutes have been made and actually played: "The experts can't believe the flute is so old and that it has technology that's been lost," Conard says. Wulf Hein, an "archaeotechnician" who reconstructed the griffin vulture bone flute using Andean condor bone, simply says, "It's marvelous." It's very easy to play, Hein says. He actually made a recording on it of "The Star-Spangled Banner" and sent it to Conard![6] Recordings made with the copies display beautiful, pure tones that sound remarkably like modern instruments. And it's amazing that the scale these flutes play is very similar to that produced by flutes made today, perhaps evidence that our human preference for certain intervals is very old. But why music? What human need did it serve even forty thousand years ago and perhaps even earlier? Of course, there's no archaeological record of the human voice, the first musical instrument. When did we begin to sing, and why? Was music an evolutionary adaptation perhaps unique to humans?

Darwin speculated that music *was* an evolutionary adaptation because a male who could sing well would have a better chance of attracting a mate.[7] Darwin wrote that "primeval man, or rather some early progenitor of man, probably used his voice largely . . . in producing true musical cadences, that is in singing." And, Darwin speculated, this power would have expressed various emotions, such as love, jealousy, triumph, and would have served as a challenge to rivals.[8]

Today, other evolutionary scientists agree with Darwin that sexual selection probably was the original motivation for music, making music directly related to survival. Proponents of this theory point to the sexiness of rock stars and other popular musicians as proof that females are still attracted to men who sing well![9] But how to account for solitary music making and enjoyment of music? Linguist and cognitive psychologist Steven Pinker believes that all the times we put on a CD when we're alone or plug into our iPod headphones argue against sexual selection being the reason for music as an evolutionary adaptation necessary for survival.

The current interest in the origins of music isn't exactly new. The questions have been asked before, but actually not so much since the late eighteenth and nineteenth centuries—Darwin's day. At that time, there was talk about the evolution of music as much as there was about the evolution of language. But then interest in the origins of language began to take precedence.

Archaeologist Steven Mithen says that even during the last thirty years as his career developed, music was rather forgotten by anthropologists. He says, "I think it may have been because it became thought to be purely a cultural phenomenon. Something to do with expertise and performance and something you could specialize in. And people had forgotten that it's much more basic than that. Something that really does pervade all stages of human life in every society." But Mithen decided that a search to find what makes humans unique must consider music. He turned to his field of expertise—the fossil record. After all, as he told me, "the one thing about the past is that it's totally silent." But an archaeologist can try to deduce from fossils what musical instruments we created and when. And then there's the human body to consider in terms of what kinds of sounds could be produced anatomically.[10]

Recently a Neanderthal skull was discovered in Israel that allowed scientists to analyze the facial structure and vocal tract. The Neanderthal skull looks remarkably similar to a human skull. And indeed we shared an ancestor just half a million years ago. Mithen says Neanderthals were probably able to make as wide a range of vocalizations as we can.

Their voices may have sounded different because they had big noses that probably gave them a more nasal quality. Some experts believe the anatomical evidence shows that this Neanderthal had language. Mithen strongly disagrees, seeing no supporting signs at all. He has a different theory.[11] "Language is a system of symbols," he says. "And there is no evidence at all for them having made any material symbols. We don't have any paintings. We don't have any carvings. We don't have any figurative art." Also, there's no indication that Neanderthals developed the kinds of more advanced tools that would have required language. Tools are an indication of cultural change that is dependent on language. Advanced tools would require people to exchange ideas and communicate about different ways to do things. Neanderthals used stone to make tools called Levallois points. But the tools remained much the same for hundreds of thousands of years. And our other ancestors, early hominids, had tools first manufactured in Africa just after one and a half million years ago. But these artifacts, Mithen says, remain just about the same for over a million years. There was no technological improvement. To Mithen that indicates their makers did not have language and neither did Neanderthals.[12]

So Mithen asked if a Neanderthal wasn't using his vocal tract for language, then what was he using it for? His answer is music. And he has a particular hypothesis about the kind of music. He believes the evolutionary question is not really about music, which can be attached to culture, but about musicality. He defines musicality as the capacity for appreciating rhythm, melody, and harmony. If Neanderthals weren't speaking a language to communicate, Mithen reasoned, then they could have been using musicality to convey ideas and emotions. He said, "They must have had a sophisticated form of communication. Just like modern humans, they would have had to have told other people how they were feeling. They would have had to look after their children and nurture them. They would have had to make plans for group hunting and general movement."[13]

Mithen imagines a kind of musical language made up of "holistic" phrases with specific meanings. He doesn't imagine each tone or note having a meaning, but rather each phrase being complete in itself. For example, there could have been a musical phrase for "let us share meat" or for "we'll go hunting."

And he thinks they were probably expressed with different pitches and rhythms. Mithen sees it as a complex, sophisticated communication system different from language or music as we know them today but having elements of both. And he believes this communication system was used not only by Neanderthals but by our direct ancestors, *Homo sapiens*, in Africa. According to Mithen:

> This is just a perfect, adaptive form of communication that evolved. And it's not half-language or half-music. It just is what it is. This is just a perfect, adaptive form of communication that evolved. The ability to use rhythm, to use variations in pitch, to develop melodies, to sing in harmony. That

comes . . . long, long before language—hundreds of thousands of years, if not millions of years before language. It's a much more basic, instinctive capacity that we have than even language itself.[14]

This system, as Mithen describes it, was what scientists call a "multimodal" form of communication, involving gesture and body movement as well as sound.

Mithen makes an appealing and imaginative case. He paints a vivid picture of the scene and sound. As I stood in the caves of southern Germany, I could imagine what he describes as these early human vocalizations in a time even before the creation of those ancient flutes.

> I think they would have probably had a lot of movement in it. Probably a lot of mime as well; telling a story or narrating something with music is very difficult. But if you combine it with mime of movement, that makes a more powerful system. I really don't want to separate sound from body movement and dance. I think they go together. And it's in our society today when we separate them, it's a really artificial separation. So as well as having these vocal tracts to make lots of audible sounds, I think Neanderthals were using their bodies for gesturing, for dancing. Then of course also making sound from their bodies, whether it's slapping their thighs or clicking their fingers. And you get fantastic sounds like . . . just swinging a bit of a skin around your head and it makes that fantastic whirling noise. So I think we see music as really a whole body experience.[15]

It's easy to believe that Neanderthal and early man made other musical sounds, by rapping stones together or using sticks or wooden spears. As they napped, or chiseled, stones to make tools, they would have been forming a beat naturally. It sounds fun—not the stuff of rigorous music lessons and exacting performances in a concert hall. And that is part of Mithen's point: "I think the way we should express it is that musicality came before language. I think that music itself is a culturally constructed entity. If you like, it's like art is a constructed entity and a different society would define art in a different way than we do."[16]

In twenty-first-century Western culture, we may have lost touch with this holistic understanding of music. Yet some cultures, even today, actually have no separate words for music and dance. And people cannot imagine hearing music without being there in person to see the movements of the music makers.

A recent study by psychologist Laurel Trainor reaffirms the close connection between the auditory and motor systems. It suggests that movement can shape how we hear. Trainor played infants a six-beat pattern that could be heard either as a waltz with the accent on the third beat or as a march with the accent on every other beat. Half of the babies were bounced on the mother's lap on every third beat, and half on every other beat. Then they were given a preference test. Both groups heard the same music with the ambiguous rhythm. The infants who'd been bounced on the third beat heard it as a waltz, and those who'd been bounced on the second beat heard it as a march. Trainor says, "So we showed a bidirectional influence. It's not only that how you hear affects how you move, but how you move affects how you hear."[17]

Sandra Trehub, who specializes in studying musical perception in infants, sees this physical aspect of music or musicality as a factor in what was probably a very important use of music by our ancestors. An infant held in the arms of a singing, dancing mother feels the vibrations of sound and the movement as all part of the experience.[18] And, of course, think of mothers singing lullabies to their babies all over the world today, cradling them and swaying to the melody and the rhythm. It's notable that lullabies have the same stepwise motion between the notes of the tune, with falling pitch contours and a narrow pitch range. They're quiet and very repetitive.

The scientists trying to make a portrait of the origins of human music making must rely on educated guesses. Some look to existing traditional societies that might give a model of earlier periods in our evolution. For instance, the Pygmies in the Congo speak in a way that seems to be a blend of musical expression and singing narrative, imitation and gesture and dance. Neuroscientist Larry Parsons calls it "a complicated mix of all these as well as language. So it's this bandwidth, this immense bandwidth."[19]

From the neuroscience perspective, Parsons and a colleague, Steven Brown, did that study to explore the origins of dance and its relationship to music and to language. As we learned, the brain scans indicated a connection between the auditory, motor, and language areas of the brain. Parsons and Brown propose a "body percussion" hypothesis for the evolution of dance. They think it began as a "sounding phenomenon": that humans generated rhythm by slapping their thighs and beating their chests.

Parsons has also done brain-imaging studies of dance. He

scanned subjects as they performed dance steps with their feet. This was the first-ever neuroscience brain-imaging study of dance. The scientists had amateur tango dancers lie flat inside a PET scanner. They listened to music through headphones and were able to move their legs along an inclined surface. In Parsons's tests, during interpretative dance there was activation in the right brain hemisphere region exactly analogous to Broca's area—the speech region—on the left. Other studies indicate this region to the right of Broca's area has to do with imitation—a key factor in learning from others and spreading culture. And, Parsons and Brown say, "just as Broca's area helps us to correctly string together words and phrases, its homologue may serve to place units of movement into seamless sequences." In other words, this area to the right of Broca's having to do with imitation deals with organizing movement in the same way that Broca's helps organize speech. These findings suggest that dance movement was a form of communication that perhaps evolved before verbal language. This experiment indicated a relationship between music, dance, and speech.

The scientists also compared scans taken when the subjects performed tango steps with the music and without music. First, Parsons and Brown compared brain activity when the dancers executed steps to the music versus merely flexing their leg muscles in time to the music without actually moving their legs. That way they could tell what brain areas were involved just in flexing but not moving the legs through space. Then they could hone in on the brain areas essential to directing the legs and creating movement patterns. The main area involved in making movement patterns was part of the parietal lobe, which contributes to spatial perception and orientation in both humans and other mammals. And the main activity of dancing to tango music was in part of the cerebellum that gets input from the spinal chord, Parsons and Brown said. "Albeit preliminary, our result lends credence to the hypothesis that this part of the cerebellum serves as a kind of conductor monitoring information across various brain regions to assist in orchestrating actions."

And with this experiment, there was a very interesting and unexpected result. The analysis showed that when the dancers were synchronizing their feet to the musical beat, a lower part of the auditory pathway, a subcortical structure called the medial geniculate nucleus, lit up. The MGN is in the lower auditory pathway and connects to the cerebellum. So it appears to help set the brain's metronome, sending information about rhythm without involving higher auditory areas in the brain. This happened only when the subjects were moving in synchrony with the beat—entraining. Therefore, Parsons and Brown think they found what's going on when we instinctively tap our feet to music—unconscious entrainment, as it's called. It is truly a very basic instinct.

Parsons and Brown wanted to explore why people dance in the first place. In many cultures, dancers put on noisemaking objects like castanets. And they think the first percussion instruments could well have been parts of dancing regalia, like the leggings worn by Aztec *danzantes* today in Mexico City. These leggings contain seeds from the ayoyote tree that cause them to make a rattling sound whenever the dancer takes a step. And even before there were these kinds of percussion instruments there was body smacking. So Parsons and Brown theorized that dance first evolved in relation to sound—music. "We have postulated a 'body percussion' hypothesis that dance evolved initially as a sounding phenomenon and that dance and music, especially percussion, evolved together as complementary ways of generating rhythm."[20]

If traditional societies are a model for early human musicality, then—Parsons points out—it may be difficult to even separate music from other elements like a kind of language and dance in terms of evolutionary adaptation. He proposed that idea to Steven Pinker, who conceded:

Language and music of course share many features. The fact that we can sing, that we can put words to music suggests that there's going to be at least a rhythmic overlap, an overlap in terms of phrasal structure. There may be some overlap in terms of auditory analysis. We live in a complex, buzzing world and our brain has to separate the wind from the animals from the voices. And it could be that the mechanisms that allow us to make sense of the auditory world also give us pleasure when they are hit by a purified, concentrated form of the most easily analyzed sounds.[21]

But Pinker still maintains that music, those sounds that give us pleasure, is a spin-off from other essential auditory skills.

The debate about "why music" really does seem to come down to whether music is seen as a specialized taste and skill or in a holistic way—as an integral part of human life, connected to other aspects of that life. And the scientists who take this approach see music in a way as its own language—as a particular kind of communication. To them, therein lies the why.

Steven Mithen comes back to traditional societies to make another point supporting his case for music as an essential part of human existence. "I can sit down and listen to the music made by Inuit Eskimos or Amazonians, and to an extent I can engage with that music. I can enjoy it. I can understand it. I can feel the same emotions they do. I can enter into their musical world. And yet, if I listen to them speak, I have no idea what they're speaking about."[22]

In the 1970s, the famous ethnomusicologist John Blacking wrote the book *How Musical Is Man?* He spoke about how music can transcend cultural constraints to become more of an experience that communicates across cultural boundaries.[23]

Mithen agrees. "Language is different. Language is about barriers. Music is about opening up and welcoming people."[24] In this view, music was first used to convey information, share emotion, soothe infants—all the ways to facilitate human interaction.

Mithen and others believe music was used to build group identity—perhaps to lead people into battle or to bring them together in worship—just as it's used today. Neuroscientist Daniel Levitin shares this view. If most people have an extraordinary memory for musical pitch, tempo, and rhythm—as he and other scientists have shown—then perhaps there was an evolutionary reason, according to Levitin. "Songs may stick in our head because they're supposed to. A lover out on a hunt for a long period of time wants to be remembered while he's away. She wants him to remember her. They have their song that they sang to each other and that sticks in the head and keeps them faithful. There are some evolutionary advantages to that."[25]

Furthermore, we now know that music affects the neural networks and structures of the brain. So neuroscience as well as conscious memory comes into play if we consider evolution and music. So does genetics. Daniel Levitin cites this revolutionary new scientific field as a fundamental argument that music was an evolutionary adaptation in humans:

I come at this from a kind of bias which is that the human genome is crowded. We only have about twenty-two or twenty-three thousand genes, and that's not a lot to do all that they have to do. The vast majority of our genes are doing kind of housekeeping functions. So if something's in there, it's there for a reason. And if music's been in there for as long as we think it has, it must be serving some evolutionary function; otherwise the genome would have kicked it out.[26]

And if music can change one brain, it can change many. How about a social group? Neuroscientists are now moving beyond the study of individual brains to that of multiple brains. Jamshed Bharucha points out that musical sound is a way to put a group of people into the same brain state. This, of course, rings true for anyone who's been transported by music—be it a rock concert or a classical symphony.

PART III

The Resonant World

CHAPTER 9

Whale Songs, Elephant Bands, and Dancing Birds

Everyone wants to understand art.
Why not try to understand the song of a bird?

—PABLO PICASSO

I t's a memorable experience to see a serious scientist dancing with a bird as part of his research. But the scientist, neurobiologist Aniruddh (Ani) Patel, is very serious indeed. He's exploring the question: Are other species musical? And Patel is not alone in pursuing this line of research, which is on the vanguard of a new field—biomusicology.

Lately scientists have wondered what the relationship is, if any, between our music and the world in which we live. Remember Larry Parsons's study of emotional reaction to birdsong. His subjects had an even greater response to birdsong in emotion areas of the brain than to human song. Parsons proposes that one possible explanation is that our ancestors heard birdsong and were inspired to create similar combinations of sounds. Biologists are actually turning to the natural world—to other species—to shed light on the role of music in human evolution. Certainly the answers to "why music" depend in part on whether music is truly unique to humans. If music exists for the sake of pleasure alone, then is that true for all species? Researchers have looked to animals to learn more about whether music is simply something beautiful we enjoy that's not necessary for survival, or something more.

Biomusicology emerged in the 1990s after decades of focus on cultural differences between musical systems and virtually no interest in an evolutionary approach to music. Now, as scientists explore the origins of human music, the investigation has inevitably expanded to look at other species and ask if they, too, may have music-like abilities. The reasoning goes that if music is an evolutionary adaptation in humans, then it should be unique to humans. So the cross-species research is crucial to scientists asking, Why music? The idea, as Ani Patel explains, is "to look for aspects of music that are particularly important for music that don't seem to be part of other cognitive domains."

Patel decided to look at rhythm—a particular aspect of rhythm. Moving to a beat, he notes, is one of the true universals of music. Every musical culture has some kind of music with a regular rhythm that people move to. And the ability to synchronize to a rhythmic beat has been thought to be one aspect of music that certainly is uniquely human. A few years ago, Patel went to Thailand to study the Thai Elephant Orchestra. The ensemble was founded by Richard Lair of the Elephant Conservation Center in Lampang and by performer/composer Dave Soldier. The idea for the orchestra arose because the people at the center noticed that when the trainers, the mahouts, played their own music the elephants seemed interested. Sixteen elephants play "music" on huge specially designed musical instruments. There are elephant-sized xylophones and drums and gongs. The animals are given mallets with which to play. Basically, they improvise, sometimes with loose cueing from a conductor. They've made several recordings.

Patel wanted to know scientifically if the elephants really were musical in any sense. He stayed with the elephants for a week, studying them and recording video. "And I definitely saw evidence that individual elephants could play rhythmically; they could play drums or cymbals with a very steady beat, without having a human sitting there tapping them on the shoulder, giving them cues. It was clear they weren't just doing this because they were being prompted."[1]

But Patel did not see any evidence that the elephants were synchronizing with each other or synchronizing to a common beat. However, they could *keep* a very steady beat individually.

Patel also observed that the elephants seemed to spontaneously play their instruments. One thirteen-year-old female, Pratidah, was the best drummer of the ensemble. Patel says she always wanted to hold the mallet a certain way, with the head pointing left. If it was given to her another way, she'd turn it around. When she hit the pair of Thai temple drums, she did so with an extremely steady tempo. It's also noteworthy that she wasn't getting any food rewards. She just responded to a "go" signal and started hitting the drum.

Patel concedes that it's anthropomorphic to say that she was enjoying her drumming. But that is how it appeared to him. And when she was playing with the whole orchestra and waiting for her cue, she would start swaying her body and trunk as if she were preparing to play.

When Patel measured the *timing* of Pratidah's drumbeats, he found they were remarkably steady. They were actually steadier than a human drumming at the same tempo. She was getting no timing cues and still was able to produce a steady rhythm.

The fact that Pratidah and the other elephants could not synchronize to a beat they heard didn't surprise Patel. Synchronization may not seem complicated to humans. But as Patel points out, dogs that have been with humans tens of thousands of years can't synchronize either. Neither can other primates.

But the story has recently become much more complicated. One thing that startled Patel and other scientists was video of a bird—a white cockatoo—that surfaced on the Internet recently. Snowball is owned by Irena Schulz and lives at a bird sanctuary in the Midwest. Schulz had discovered that when she played music with a strong rhythmic beat, Snowball would dance up a storm, lifting and tapping his legs and bobbing his head—apparently in perfect time. Schulz—a former scientist—had never noticed behavior like this from a bird. The video came to the attention of Ani Patel. His interest in looking at possible musical synchronization in other species drove him to collaborate with Snowball's owner to do some tests. He and his colleagues were very curious indeed:

We thought, is this real? Well, it's real. He really does dance to music and he's not just imitating the movement of his owner. You can be still and not be giving it cues and the bird will still dance. Can he dance to other songs? He does. Can he adjust his tempo to the same song if you make it faster or slower, so it's a version he's never heard before? And the answer is yes. Within a limited range he can do that. This is real synchronization; this is real musical synchronization. And this shows that this ability is not something you need a human brain that has been specifically shaped by evolution for music to do.[2]

So Patel is saying that neither cockatoos nor humans probably evolved a specific musical ability as an adaptation; instead, music may have developed along with other abilities, he proposes. Cockatoos are one of the species of birds that have what's called vocal learning. That is, they have brain circuits that enable them to learn songs and to vocalize. Humans have vocal learning. Other primates do not. Patel speculates that vocal-learning birds like Snowball may respond to music because they already have the neural networks enabling them to vocalize, to coordinate the motor and auditory systems, and make complex sound patterns. It's the same argument he and others use to say that human response to music is a spin-off from other mental abilities. Chimps, our closest relatives, do not have vocal learning, so Patel is willing to bet that they can't be taught to synchronize to a beat.

Patel observed that Snowball, the cockatoo who can keep a beat, actually seems to enjoy dancing. He doesn't get any kind of food reward. And he likes doing it *with* someone. Patel tried dancing with him and said:

> It's remarkable. This bird really does seem to enjoy it. I mean, I never thought in my scientific career I would be dancing with a cockatoo. But hey, I'll go wherever the research takes me. One thing I noticed was this bird really wanted eye contact. He cared that I was dancing with him and that I was looking at him. And actually, at one point I turned around [to] see what happens if I continue dancing . . . still right next to him, but I turned around and looked the other way. And his owner, who was watching this experiment, said he [Snowball] just kind of stopped and looked around as if—what's happening? Why isn't this guy, you know, facing me and dancing with me?[3]

Patel thinks that part of what's going on with this behavior is that there's a social component. And that's amazing, he says:

> So this animal is opening up a whole bunch of new questions to me and to, I think, other people in the field. What is the interaction between brain circuits that are involved in moving to a beat and brain circuits that are involved in social cognition? We think that having this complex vocal learning is the foundation. But then on top of that, you need the ability to imitate, because some birds learn their songs but they learn only their own species' song and then that's it; they don't tend to learn other songs. But cockatoos and other animals like this can actually imitate other sounds,

and they also imitate the movements of others. And so, is that another level of brain circuitry that you need to get this kind of synchronization going between humans when they respond to music? So it's layering and enriching our understanding of this basic human behavior.[4]

When I asked Patel whether it is possible that both we and other species could be "wired" for music, he responded:

That is a good question. You might argue that this shows that cockatoos have been shaped for music, just as humans have been shaped for music. And it's true that animals that have complex vocal communication signals—we call them songs—say when birds sing. So isn't that, in a sense, music? But if you look more closely at what animals do with their vocalizations there are lots of things about them that I think are different from music. Animals tend to use their vocalizations for specific functional reasons. Male birds typically sing to attract a mate or to defend a territory.[5]

Patel notes that birds typically sing in the spring when there are certain hormonal and neural changes in the brain. Humans make music year-round and for many purposes. He concludes that the acoustic displays of animals like birds and whales are fundamentally different from what we humans consider music. Regarding Snowball and his ability for musical synchronization, Patel comes back to his basic argument. "If a bird can do something that we think of as genuinely musical, like moving to the beat of music, to me that suggests that that doesn't require natural selection for music, because that bird has never had what I think of as full-blown music as part of its ecology, as part of its behavior, and yet it can do something that we think of as musical."[6]

Patel is not alone in believing that the music-like sounds of other species are not truly music. Neuropsychologist Isabelle Peretz is convinced that "only humans have a natural, or innate, inclination to engage with music."[7] Of course birds and other species like whales do use sound to communicate with each other. The issue is whether these sounds are music. Neuroscientist Robert Zatorre points out that bats can do echolocation; humans cannot, but we don't need to. "Our need is to communicate with others socially. And we do so with music and language," Zatorre says. "And that's maybe the most characteristically human of abilities." Zatorre argues that it's "misplaced" to say that animal music-like sounds are actually analogous to human music. They sound like music to us, but that's anthropomorphic, Zatorre says. Birdsong is pleasing to us. But birds use song to find mates and defend territory. So do frogs, Zatorre continues, "but no one talks about frog croaks as a musical ability, right?"[8]

So from this perspective, the communicative music-like sounds of other species are really more like language. Yet, in the last decade or so, a growing number of experts are beginning to question the conviction that music is only human. Certainly, a growing number of researchers are doing studies to gather evidence for the debate.

Birdsong scientists, as a group, are divided on the question as to whether this is music. They analyze the song structure, searching for clues to why and how birds sing. Ofer Tcher-nichovski, a neuroscientist and head of the Laboratory of Ani-mal Behavior at City University of New York's City College, studies sound production in songbirds with special focus on the zebra finch. He records their songs and finds amazing struc-ture. A sonogram shown in closeup and with the audio played slowly reveals the melodic shape of a zebra finch song (see page 11 in the color insert). It has a theme or motif and different syl-lables. And there's a vibrato at a certain point and a glissando.[9]

About that glissando, Tchernichovski remarks, "Look how beautifully it goes down. Those are two harmonic sounds. That's musical terminology." Tchernichovski further explains:

I don't know if birdsong and music songs are the same. But I think they share something. Maybe it's not scientific to ask if songs are beautiful, but as a scientist, I like to fol-low beauty. On a personal level, I think that the songs are very beautiful. They're very appealing. And I don't think that's a coincidence. But what is it about? The scientific question about it is: Let's try, first of all, to see that hidden beauty.[10]

So rather than ask directly if birds are merely making sounds to attract mates or defend territory, Tchernichovski studies the development of birdsong—in a species and in individual birds as they mature and learn their songs. His experiments show how the bird can convert sounds that it hears into motor ges-tures of the complex vocal organs that are at the back of its chest. The two vocal organs each have six sets of muscles that sit near the heart. Tchernichovski notes that "they don't sing from the throat. They sing from just above the heart."[11] The bird manipulates those muscles and airflow through the vocal organs to match the memory of a song of a bird tutor that the bird might have heard even as long as a year ago.

One hears in the way he speaks that Tchernichovski is truly awestruck and emotionally moved by these songs. "When you listen to a song, a song is like a crystal. It has a repeating structure. A zebra finch sings the same song again and again. A nightingale can sing two hundred songs, but it still sings them again and again."[12]

Erich Jarvis, a birdsong scientist at Duke University, found what's probably a marker of vocal learning—what are called differential gene regulations identified in the vocal brain areas of songbirds. Jarvis says these gene regulations actually protect the speech and singing areas of the brain that become active in vocal learners.

Tchernichovski is conducting some studies of nightingale song along with David Rothenberg, a musician and author who has studied and written about birdsong and whale song. Rothenberg is completely convinced that it's correct to call birdsong music. And he's used to responding to his critics. "People sometimes say, 'Rothenberg doesn't believe that male birds sing to attract mates and defend territory.' It's not true. It's not that I don't believe that. If that's what the song is for. But that's not what the song *is*. What is it? It's really music."

Rothenberg often plays his clarinet with birds and feels the birds are really interacting musically. He first became interested in birdsong when he came across sonograms—the technology birdsong scientists like Tchernichovski use to see structure in sounds. Rothenberg is particularly taken by the song of the veery, a small thrush. The sonogram shows a repeating pattern in four parts (see the color insert). Rothenberg says he slows down the sonogram so the human ear can hear the structure more clearly. And sure enough I did hear the pattern the sonogram depicts visually. Rothenberg remarks, "A birdsong slowed down like this, you really hear why birdsong is music. It doesn't just sound like music. It really is musical utterance. Why do I say that? Because it's a pattern of sounds with a beginning, middle, and end."[13]

And Rothenberg has transcribed the veery song into musical notation (see below).

Rothenberg is making his point that birdsong is not exactly language—just as music is not the same as our language. Music may have syntax, but it doesn't have a complicated meaning hidden in the syntax. And birdsong—like human music—has its own meaning, unlike the simple calls birds use to convey specific ideas such as "I'm hungry" or "Danger." Birds know these calls from birth, Rothenberg points out, but they *learn* their songs as they mature—even though they're wired to learn their species' own songs.

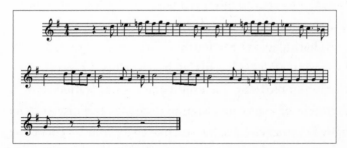

FIGURE 3 Veery song transcribed into musical notation. CREDIT: DAVID ROTHENBERG

He explains that the grammar and syntax of birdsong is not symbolic; it does have a simple meaning. "If you look at a piece by Bach, an instrumental by Mozart or Coltrane," he says, "you can't say what all those notes mean. You can't translate it into words. And that's why birdsong, I believe, has meanings in the same way."

Famous composers including Mozart and Olivier Messiaen have incorporated birdsong into their works. Mozart borrowed a tune from his pet starling in his K. 522 Divertimento, "A Musical Joke," composed eight days after the bird died. Ornithologists speculate that Mozart recognized that the starling, which had two vocal chambers, was actually singing two tunes at once in counterpoint. Hence, the dissonance in Mozart's rendition. Beethoven also used the blackbird song in a rondo of a violin concerto. And Messiaen probably used birdsong more than any other composer did. All of these musical greats evidently heard a kind of music in birdsong and would likely agree with Rothenberg.

Ofer Tchernichovski decided to collaborate with David Rothenberg on the nightingale song study. They combined a musical approach with the scientific by looking at the types of sounds and rhythms in sonograms of nightingale songs (see the color insert). Nightingales have hundreds of different songs and rhythms.

Tchernichovski has found in birdsongs some equivalents to musical scales. Also, his lab has developed a way to analyze rhythm in birdsong. He uses a graphic illustration showing a hierarchy of sounds and rhythms (see the color insert). When a baby bird makes calls, it looks like chaos—just a collection of unorganized sounds. But as the bird grows, you can see a struc-

ture forming, with elements that are like syllables. Tchernichovski says that "generally the process you see is how a cloud
of unstructured sounds develop structure like a crystal emerging. So the syntax, what they call syntax in song, is order of
sounds. And rhythm is really the time domain implementation
of syntax."

The nightingale song has been regaled in poetry and prose
through the ages. We humans love listening to it. So does that
mean that the nightingale and other bird species are vocalizing
in terms to which the human brain really does respond in the
same way it responds to human music? Tchernichovski thinks
to some extent that might be true. But he, too, reminds us that
scientists cannot be sure that what sounds like music to our
ear is truly music to the bird.

David Rothenberg wonders, Why all those complex patterns
in birdsong? Why does a nightingale need to sing for an hour?
Is there some reason a bird sings beyond attracting a mate or
defending territory? Could he be singing just for the sheer
pleasure? He says he's noticed when he plays his clarinet with
birds that they just keep singing and singing. They don't seem
to want to stop. And in fact, there's now hard science that sheds
light on this question of whether birdsong is pleasurable to the
birds that produce it.[14]

Erich Jarvis, a neurobiologist at Duke University, has discovered that dopamine, a hormone associated with pleasure responses, is released in the brains of songbirds when they sing.
He explains that in all vertebrates there's a midbrain region
called the VTA (ventral tegmental area) that sends a strong
projection of dopamine to another area called the striatum,

another brain region vertebrates all share. Studies over the last thirty years have led to two theories that might explain what's going on with dopamine releases. The first is that dopamine is the "feel-good drug" of the brain—a reward drug, in scientific terms. The second hypothesis is that dopamine reinforces learning behavior because it controls synaptic interactions. If you get a good result from an interaction between neurons, your brain experiences something and dopamine is released. This then strengthens the connections because the organism associates that activity with pleasure and will therefore do it again and again.

Jarvis inserted probes in the vocal part of the striatum in songbirds while they sang, and he found that more dopamine was released during singing. Moreover, it was released at higher levels when the bird was singing to a female than by itself. So the birds *are* singing to attract a mate and they feel good in the process. They're enjoying singing and will do it again, making it more likely that they'll attract a mate, reproduce, and continue the species.[15]

There's other intriguing evidence indicating that some other species may be able to feel emotion beyond just pleasure caused by a dopamine release. Patrick Hof, a neuroscientist at the Mount Sinai School of Medicine in New York City, has discovered a special kind of neuron called a spindle cell. In the brains of animals, these cells are associated with the ability to feel emotion. Spindle cells in humans are large neurons found in two areas of the cerebral cortex that activate in situations involving reactions of pleasure or disgust, responses to particular social contexts, and moral judgments. If a mother is shown a picture of her child, the spindle cells in the left side of these regions activate. If a person is shown a photo of something scary, the spindle cells on the right side activate. So these regions combined serve as a command-and-control center for the autonomic nervous system involved in emotional response.

Significantly, Hof has also found spindle cells in the brains of certain other mammals: Elephants have them. Humpback whales have them.[16] These are large-brained mammals and they have a high degree of social organization. However, some other larger-brained mammals like gibbons—at least those tested so far—do not seem to have spindle cells. Neither do macaque monkeys or baboons, which are also extremely social. So socialization may be connected to some degree with the existence of spindle cells in a species.

Hof believes the development of spindle cells also has to do with the evolution of certain brain functions that have to do with the sense of self and the body, that is, how an individual feels inside of himself—happy, for instance. Bonobos, he says, clearly have this ability.[17] And researchers at the Great Ape Trust in Iowa have an ongoing project exploring the musical appreciation and abilities of language-trained bonobos. A few years back, the British rock star Peter Gabriel and his group jammed with the bonobos, who seemed to enjoy the musical exchange.

Consider the humpback whale, the most prolific "singer" in the ocean. Perhaps spindle cells help explain their "songs." They have very long, complex vocalizations. In a 1971 issue of the journal *Science* (cover article),[18] the scientists Roger Payne and Scott McVay published what would prove to be a seminal paper about their study of humpback songs. They wrote that they felt justified in calling them songs according to the definition of song as "a series of notes, generally of more than one type, uttered in succession and so related as to form a recognizable sequence or pattern in time." Payne and McVay did the first in-depth analysis of recorded humpback songs. They noted the form of the sounds using spectrographic analysis and some-times simple shorthand. When they diagrammed the songs, they found they were highly structured, with a range of notes that spanned over six octaves and with six "themes, phrases that repeat." Like our music, whale songs have structure, rhyth-mic variations, harmony, and pitch relationships. Musician/ composer Paul Winter has even arranged whale songs for hu-man instruments.

As Payne and McVay explain in the paper, the spectrogram analysis (figure 4) shows two complete songs (1 and 2). Fre-quency and time scales are indicated. The left side is a tracing of the spectrograms on the right, emphasizing loud notes of the song and leaving out extraneous noise in the ocean.

Male humpback whales produce songs during mating sea-son. They consist of a variety of both low- and high-frequency moans and cries that are repeated over many hours. The songs, which can travel thousands of kilometers underwater, can be recorded underwater using hydrophones.

Humpbacks are vocal learners, meaning that like zebra finches and other songbirds they have the ability to imitate and learn songs. Dolphins, which are actually small whales, also have this ability. Whales and dolphins also have social organi-zation. Humpbacks are communicators. They can sing for up to twenty-four hours at a time. The phrases are repeated over and over again, rather like rhyme.

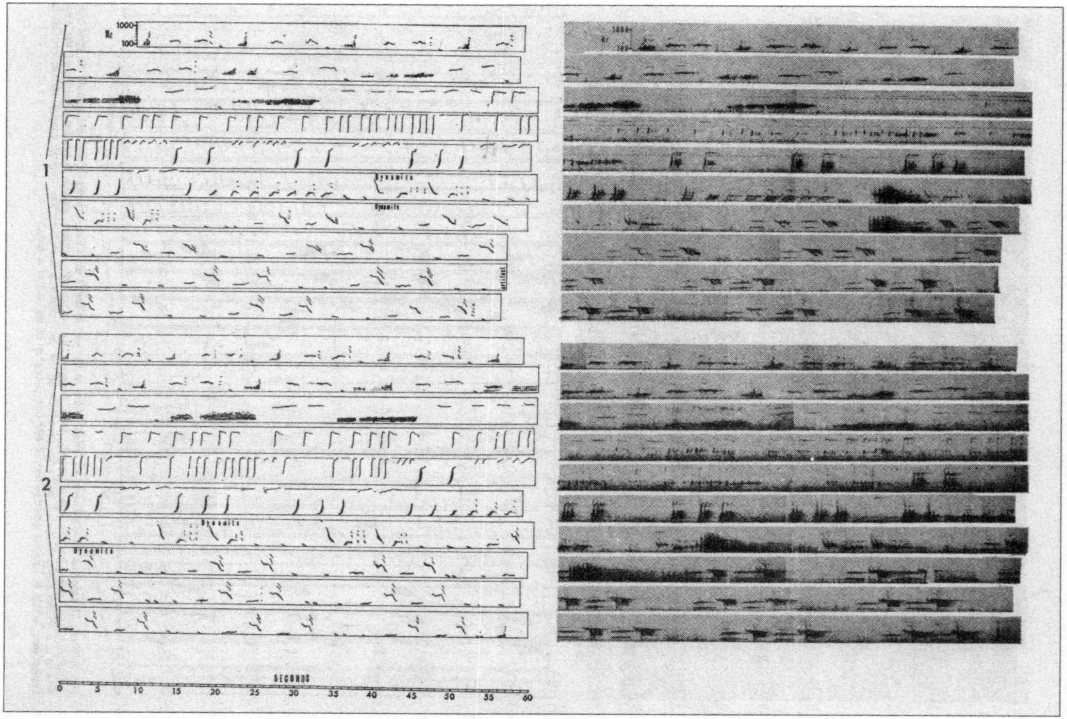

FIGURE 4 Spectograms of humpback whale song. CREDIT: SCOTT MCVAY AND ROGER PAYNE

Scott McVay confesses that the humpback vocalizations initially sounded to him like a cacophony of sound. But after a few weeks, he and Payne figured out the pattern. And it turns out all the whales they analyzed were singing the same song, which can last from six to thirty minutes.[19] Later, researcher Katy Payne (also a whale researcher, then married to Roger) discovered that the songs evolve over time, so that within a span of four to six years, all the humpback whales in all the oceans are singing a totally different song. This is true of the song cycles in the Atlantic, Pacific, and Indian Oceans.[20]

So why are they singing? McVay and Payne said in their paper that it might have something to do with attracting a female. But, as McVay points out, to date there's been no evidence, on film or in any other way, that a female has been drawn by the singing! So maybe, McVay says, the song has something to do with the hierarchy among males. But he also comes back to an observation made in the paper. "We have become aware of what we believe to be the humpbacks' most extraordinary feature— they emit a series of surprisingly beautiful sounds, a phenomenon that has not been reported previously in more than a passing way."[21]

Scientists like McVay and Ofer Tchernichovski readily spoke of their own response to the sounds of other species in terms of their intellectual and emotional reaction to beauty. In fact, it was remarkable, McVay notes, that this observation of beauty was accepted for publication in a scientific journal. McVay, who majored in English literature, hears poetry in the song of the humpback.

Scott McVay wrote a poem about whale song, back when he

was working on that groundbreaking paper. In "Whale Sing," he says:

> *Up and up and up the scale*
> > *beyond the topmost upper note*
> > *and beyond that*
> > *straining for ultimates*
> *leaving a low wailing*
> > *a small sob before*
> > > *and beneath*
> *to the reachingest next-to-god note of all,*
> *a Humpback sings his song.*
> *The Song of Songs.*
> *The Hymn of Hymns.*

Science, McVay says, "is doing some kind of bean counting, looking for patterns. With poetry, you let the floodgates reveal how you are responding on a very subjective, full-throated scale."

McVay is very much the scientist. But he wants others to hear the poetry—and the music—in the song of the humpback:

> It would appear that in the natural world there is this propensity for communicating and communicating in the best way possible within the constraints of that frame of reference . . . The point is when you get a master like Bach or Shakespeare or Goethe, or the humpback whale, it seems like there's the impetus within life to communicate. Sometimes it's subtle. Sometimes it's raucous. Sometimes it's beautiful.

But it is profoundly affecting within the domain of that species to communicate among themselves.[22]

The recent research in the field of biomusicology is letting us hear a whole new world of music-like sounds produced by other species. It turns out even mice "sing." Perhaps thankfully, we can't hear it because the frequency is too high. But neurobiologists Tim Holy and Zhongsheng Guo at Washington University School of Medicine in Missouri analyzed recordings of the sounds mice make when they encounter sex pheromones of potential mates.[23] When analyzed, the researchers deciphered what they heard as songs with rhythm, and repeating syllables, like "the twittering of a bird," Tim Holy said.

Erich Jarvis recently completed a study on mouse ultrasonic songs that males sing to females. Erich Jarvis—whose focus had been birdsong—then did a study to determine if the mice have vocal learning, like songbirds. He found they do—to a limited degree. Jarvis calls this "a milestone kind of story." He says this discovery of song production and vocal learning in mice could mean that vocal learning is a continuum in evolution. But there's much more research to be done.[24]

David Rothenberg's investigation of bird- and whale song has led him to believe that each species has a particular way of using sound. He says, "I really like this idea of Darwin's that each species has its aesthetic—that they had certain kinds of sounds they like."[25]

Other species besides songbirds and cetaceans sing together. It's recently been found that several do synchronized singing.

The only primate species other than humans that shows signs of *synchronized* vocalization is the gibbon. Gibbons sing in pairs with a melodious call. A study in Cambodia determined that this seems to be a bonding device but only between pairs.[26] The study also showed that the sounds were specific to whether there was a predator or a neutral stimulus. That is, the *sequence* of sounds was specific to the stimulus. So to neuroscientist Larry Parsons that means "for the first time there's another animal species that can use wordlike semantic units and string them together in different sequences."[27] In other words, he's saying this finding could challenge the theory that humans are the only primates with language.

Another study[28] shows that plain-tailed wrens—a kind of songbird—sing synchronized choruses among birds that live together in small colonies. The males sing for about two seconds and then the females alternate. A team of researchers led by Peter Slater, a biology professor at the University of St. Andrews, Scotland, heard this vocalizing in an Ecuadorian bamboo forest. Slater notes, "It's already known that some birds duet and that others sing in choruses, but these wrens do both, and furthermore, the choruses are extraordinarily precise and well coordinated." The birds sing about twenty sets of phrases. The males sing in unison. They pause. Then the females pick up. They are virtuosos. It's probably, along with whale song, the most extravagant display of song in a non-human species.

Why do these wrens sing? There's that question again. Slater thinks it could be a form of defense against other members of their own species. The singing could also help synchronize breeding, Slater believes.[29] Larry Parsons speculates that the wren song is another example of a species using song for socialization—social bonding.[30]

The answer to the question as to whether the sounds, the songs, of other species are "music" may be subjective. But now a significant number of new scientific studies are investigating the assumption that other species have no music-like abilities. A number of them are actually challenging that assumption.

There's one line of research aimed at determining if other species appreciate human music. Stravinsky once remarked that his music was "best understood by children and animals." But what evidence is there that other species really respond to *any* of our music?

Consider the ability to recognize pitch. It had been thought that only humans can recognize and respond to a melody. Experiments show that when you play a tune to zebra finches or starlings—or capuchin monkeys in one study—and then transpose it up or down an octave, the animals do not recognize the song. But in 2000, a study by Anthony Wright and his colleagues at the University of Texas Medical School became one of the first to start a new line of investigation. That's because Wright and his team found that rhesus monkeys *could* transpose melodies by octaves. Still, they could do this only when they were tested on songs like "Happy Birthday" with strong transitions in tones—that is, strong melodies. Wright thinks he got this result because earlier experiments used either atonal music or notes with no melody.[31]

More recently, other researchers have pursued the investigation with monkeys. In Japan, Tasuku Sugimoto and Kazuhide Hashiya tested how a young captive chimpanzee, Sakura, responded to music as she grew from seventeen to twenty-three weeks old. Sakura had been abandoned by her mother and had never heard any kind of music before the experiment. As she listened to various melodies she could pull on a cord that would cause the music to be repeated. During six trials, the researchers played a variety of consonant and dissonant, less pleasant-sounding, music—at least in human terms. Across all six sessions, Sakura pulled the cord more often for the consonant, pleasant-sounding music. Remember the studies with human infants found that they preferred consonance. The Japanese researchers wrote that "the preference for human music over dissonant music in an infant chimpanzee has implications for the debate surrounding human uniqueness in the capacity for music appreciation."[32] Still, Sakura was not given the choice of silence rather than music.

When it comes to pitch recognition, there's even been a study with the carp. Ava Chase at the Rowland Institute at Harvard did a study showing that carp can actually tell the difference between baroque music and John Lee Hooker. She gave them a button to press with their snouts to indicate their recognition.[33] And java sparrows can distinguish between Bach and Schoenberg. Shigeru Watanabe at Keio University in Tokyo found they could learn differences between classical and more modern music and could distinguish between Vivaldi and Elliott Carter. They preferred the more tonal, harmonious melodies of Vivaldi. In this study, the birds were given a choice of silence and still chose the pleasant-sounding music.[34]

But some scientists have raised the question as to whether these tests with human music really tell the whole story about preferences and emotional response to music in other species. If each species, as Scott McVay and David Rothenberg believe, has its own way of using sound, might it not appreciate its own sounds or "music" more than human music?

American researchers Charles Snowdon and David Teie recently published a paper reporting an experiment with tamarin monkeys. They found that while the tamarins were indifferent to the sound of human music, they responded with more arousal to music based on tamarin vocalizations. The researchers described how they created "music" based on tamarin sounds: "We used a musical analysis of the tamarin vocal repertoire to identify common prosodic melodic structures and tempos in tamarin calls that were related to specific behavioral contexts." They used fear/threat–based vocalizations and also more calming vocalizations. Both contained the frequency range and tempos of tamarins. So these scientists concluded that "the tempos and pitch ranges of human music may not be relevant for another species." But just as music has an emotional effect on humans, so—Snowdon and Teie propose—the "music" of other species can impact them in a similar way. They actually propose that the elements of music—pitch, timbre, and tempo—"can specifically alter affective, behavioral and physiological states in infant and adult humans as well as companion animals."[35]

Whether you have a tamarin monkey at home or a dog or cat, the music you play can matter to them. Of course no one has gotten to the point of composing music based on dog and cat sounds. However, CDs that alter human music to appeal to companion animals is being marketed.

So where do the recent studies leave us in terms of the musi-

Bobby McFerrin singing. (*The Music Instinct: Science & Song*, PBS)

Percussionist Dame Evelyn Glennie, who is profoundly deaf, feels sound through her feet and other parts of her body. (James Wilson/© Evelyn Glennie)

Hair cells in the inner ear convert vibrations of different frequencies into neural signals sent to the brain stem. (Susumu Nishinaga/Photo Researchers, Inc., image SF 7592. Used by permission.)

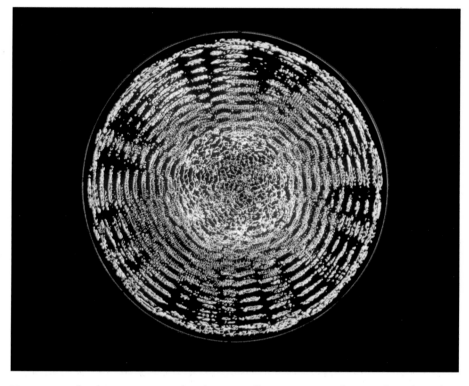

Using new technology to transmit the vibrations of music to water, photographer Alexander Lauterwasser photographed the pattern of a monochord with overtone singing. (*Cymatics: A Study of Wave Phenomena and Vibration*, copyright © 2004 MACROmedia Publishing, Newmarket, NH, USA. www.cymaticsource.com. Used by permission.)

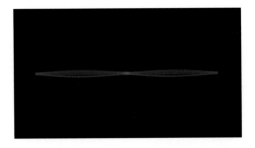

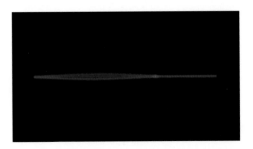

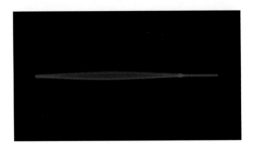

If you divide a string in half by plucking it, you are playing an octave (top). Divide the string so that two thirds of it vibrates and you get a fifth (middle). If three quarters of it vibrates, you have a fourth (bottom). (*The Music Instinct: Science & Song*, PBS)

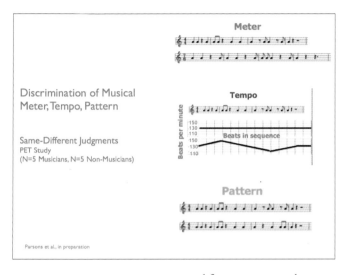

Neuroscientist Lawrence Parsons tested five musicians and five non-musicians to study what areas of the brain are activated by music's meter, tempo, and pattern (melody). (Lawrence M. Parsons)

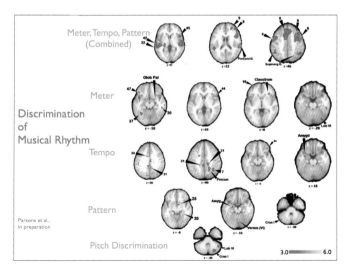

Parsons's PET scans study shows that distinct areas of the brain are activated by various musical elements. (Lawrence M. Parsons)

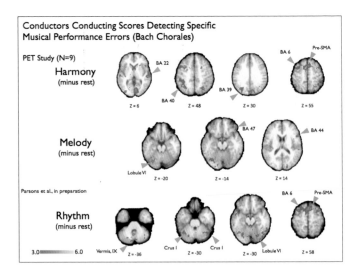

Conductors Conducting Scores Detecting Specific
Musical Performance Errors (Bach Chorales)

PET Study (N=9)

Harmony
(minus rest)

BA 22
BA 6
Pre-SMA
BA 40
BA 39

Z = 6   Z = 48   Z = 30   Z = 55

Melody
(minus rest)

BA 47
BA 44
Lobule VI

Z = -20   Z = -14   Z = 14

Parsons et al., in preparation

Rhythm
(minus rest)

BA 6
Pre-SMA
Crus I
Crus I
Lobule VI

3.0 ▬ 6.0   Vermis, IX   Z = -36   Z = -30   Z = -30   Z = 58

PET scan results of Lawrence Parsons's study of brain activity
of orchestra conductors as they process music. (Lawrence M.
Parsons)

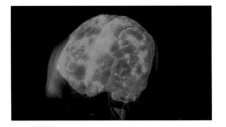

The brain processes all elements of
music—rhythm, pitch, tempo, etc.—
and puts them together to form music.
So many areas of the brain are involved
that one could say we have a veritable
"brain orchestra" in our head. (*The Music
Instinct: Science & Song*, PBS)

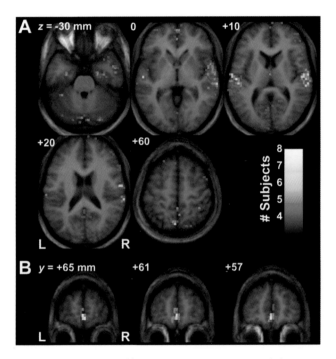

Using brain imaging of listeners, Petr Janata mapped those brain areas activated by tonality tasks. A shows areas activated. B shows that the only areas whose activity patterns were significantly and consistently correlated across listeners were the rostral portion of the ventromedial superior frontal gyrus and the right orbitofrontal gyrus—regions of the prefrontal cortex. (Petr Janata)

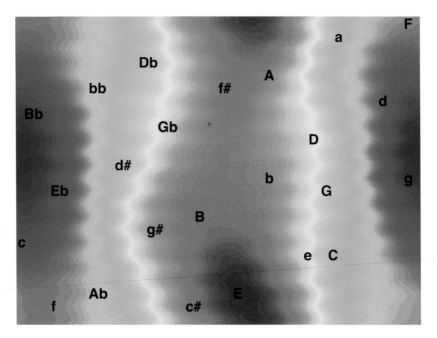

Still image from animation of how music moves around in tonal space. The letters correspond to the 24 Major and minor keys in Western music. As the harmonies change, so does the color and activation pattern. (Petr Janata)

Tom Fritz (right) in Cameroon in 2005 with members of the Mafa tribe listening to Western music for the first time. (Ildiko Hetesi)

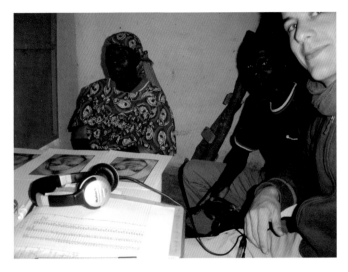

Mafa tribe members, unaccustomed to Western music, listened to various melodies through headphones and were able to identify whether the music was happy, sad, or scary by pointing to a photograph of a face displaying the corresponding emotion. (Tom Fritz)

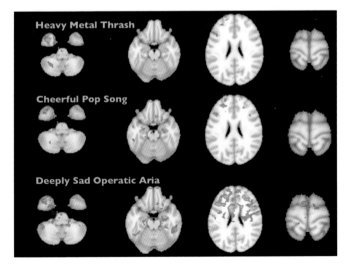

Lawrence Parsons's fMRI brain scan of a subject listening to Richard Strauss's *Four Last Songs.* (Lawrence M. Parsons)

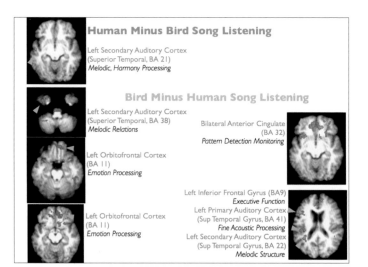

Images from Lawrence Parsons's study of brain response of people listening to human song and birdsong (top) and listening solely to human song or birdsong (bottom). (Lawrence M. Parsons)

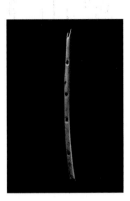

A five-finger-hole flute, carved from the radius of a griffin vulture, discovered in 2009 by archeologist Nicolas Conard and colleagues at the University of Tuebingen, Germany. (Hilde Jensen, copyright © University Tuebingen)

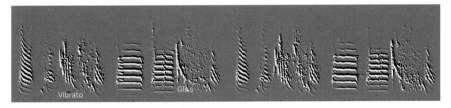

Sonogram showing the melodic shape of a zebra finch song, with vibrato and glissando identified. (Ofer Tchernichovski)

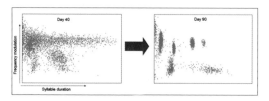

A graphic illustration of the development of birdsong structure, plotting frequency modulation (y-axis) and syllable duration (x-axis), from day 40 to day 90. A baby bird's calls are chaotic; however, as the bird grows, its calls develop musical elements, similar to syllables and syntax. (Ofer Tchernichovski)

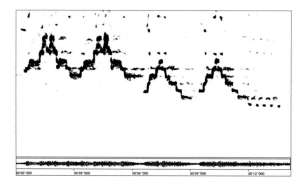

Sonogram of the birdsong of a veery. (David Rothenberg)

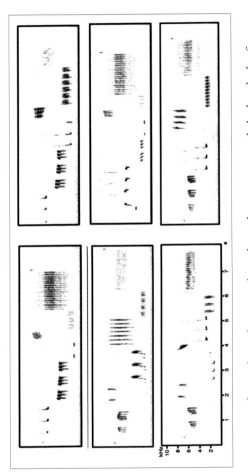

Sonograms of six nightingale songs. The nightingale's repertoire includes hundreds of songs and rhythms. (David Rothenberg)

This image was produced by converting the sound frequencies of a humpback whale song using a mathematical process known as wavelets. Wavelets reveal structure and detail not always visible in standard graphs of frequency over time. (Image created by Mark Fischer from Aguasonic Acoustics, USA. Aguasonic Acoustics/Science Photo Library)

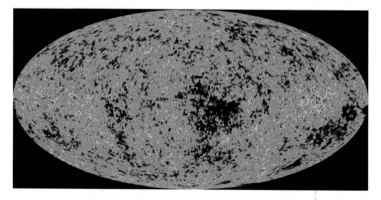

An image of Cosmic Microwave Background (CMB) radiation, first detected in 1965 through a radio antenna. In 2003 NASA's Wilkinson Microwave Anisotropy Probe (WMAP) satellite produced an extremely sensitive all-sky map of the CMB which, when cleaned and contrast enhanced, reveals the slight patchiness coming from glowing sound waves that become, over time, galaxies and stars. (NASA WMAP Satellite)

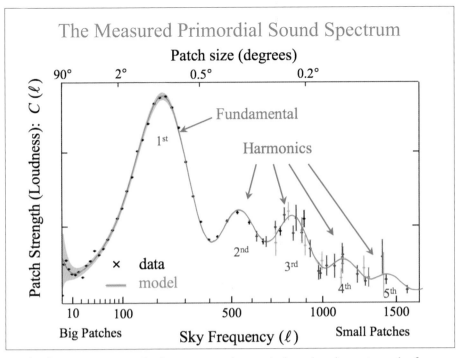

The Measured Primordial Sound Spectrum

Patch size (degrees)

Patch Strength (Loudness): C (ℓ)

Fundamental

1st

Harmonics

2nd

3rd

4th 5th

× data
— model

90°   2°   0.5°   0.2°

10   100   500   1000   1500

Big Patches   Sky Frequency (ℓ)   Small Patches

Graph of cosmic acoustics. The data points in this graph show the relative strength of different-size patches measured from observations of the microwave background, while the solid line shows the predictions of a sophisticated computer simulation of the young universe. The observations span a range of patch sizes from large ones, spanning a quarter of the sky, to small ones, of which five would fit under the full moon. These correspond to waves in the early universe from 45 million light-years across to 20,000 light-years across, while only those smaller than 220,000 light-years are in fact true sound waves. (Mark Whittle, University of Virginia: www.astro.virginia.edu~dmw86/BBA)

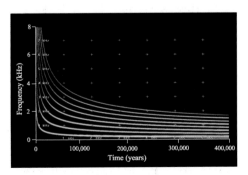

This graph, made by Mark Whittle, shows how the pitch of the primordial sound (y-axis, upshifted by 50 octaves) changes across the first 400 thousand years (x-axis). The sound loudness is color coded (top bar), with black as quiet and red as loud. Notice how the fundamental and harmonics all drop rapidly across the first 400 thousand ($10^{\wedge 5}$) years, and then drop more steadily, getting louder, out to 400 thousand ($4 \times 10^{\wedge 5}$) years. The overall impression of this sound is a "descending scream." (Mark Whittle, University of Virginia: www.astro.virginia.edu~dmw86/BBA)

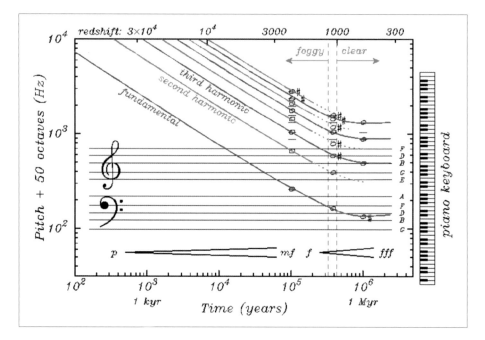

A graph using musical notation to map the evolution of cosmic sound over the first 400,000 years after the Big Bang. (Mark Whittle, University of Virginia: www.astro.virginia .edu˜dmw86/BBA)

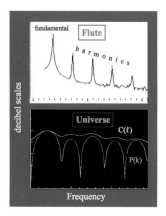

Comparison of the narrow harmonics of a flute and the broad harmonics of cosmic sound. (Flute harmonics graph by Joe Wolfe used by permission. Cosmic harmonics graph by Mark Whittle: www.astro.virginia.edu˜dmw86/BBA)

cality of animals? We still don't know completely what these vocalizations mean to each species. And we don't know what's really going on when a java sparrow, for example, chooses Vivaldi over Carter. Are they discerning the difference in the same way we do?

Human music assuredly is more complex than the "songs" of other animals. That's why it's possible for some scientists to argue that it is closely linked to language and may even have been the precursor to language. But the research with songbirds and gibbons suggests their music-like vocalizations also may be used in a communicative way.

Perhaps music and language could be linked in other species as well as in humans. In songbirds, Erich Jarvis found the pathways for song are comparable to the human brain pathways for language.[36] And recently Jarvis completed other studies with fascinating genetic evidence that humans and vocal-learning mammals as well as songbirds share a set of mutations in genes involved in brain connectivity that link vocal learning to motor control—thereby enabling song production.[37] Jarvis is very excited about this discovery because the genetic information confirms similar music-like song production across species. "What's so remarkable for me," says Jarvis, "is that there is convergence of these gene mutations in multiple genes in several pathways in the same locations among species. So we're seeing convergence at the behavioral level with vocal learning and singing and convergence in the brain and at the molecular level."[38]

He thinks these gene mutations go way back in time. The Neanderthal genome is now available and we've learned that the same mutations have been found in Neanderthal genes—a clear indication that the Neanderthal, too, had vocal learning and sang. These findings certainly seem to support Steven Mithen's theory of a "singing Neanderthal."

Jarvis's recent studies have confirmed that the brain pathways controlling singing and the ability to learn how to sing in both humans and songbirds are all embedded in an ancient motor pathway found in all vertebrates. The motor pathway involves seven brain regions and gets input from both the visual and auditory pathways. The motor pathway actually duplicated itself and hooked up in the brain stem of the embryo with the neurons that control vocalization. So Jarvis thinks this is the story of the evolution of vocal learning— the duplication of these pathways so they could connect.[39] In sum, the Jarvis genetic research adds fuel to the argument that some other species, like humans, have a musicality that's linked to movement and language.

We are still somewhat in the realm of speculation here. And the research with other species is ongoing. Yet as I listened with Larry Parsons to the "songs" of mice and wrens and gibbons and whales, I understood the speculation. When the frequencies are altered—as David Rothenberg does comparing bird- and whale song—it's impossible not to hear the similarities, the patterns.

David Rothenberg believes that "there is in some sense a pattern rhythm and form in the music of the animal world that is common at different levels of organization. I would say that just as people have identified different visual patterns in the visual world, the way plants have developed a certain sense of order and symmetry, that the same thing is going on in sound."

Rothenberg finds the patterns of music-like sound a way to communicate across species.[40]

I come back yet again to the question that is being asked: Do other species enjoy music—theirs and ours—in some way, beyond the purposes of attracting a mate and defending territory? Could it be, after all, that both humans and other species evolved for music, maybe just for its own sake, for pleasure and beauty?

To McVay, and other researchers exploring the use of sound by other species, we can hear the universal in these "songs" of fellow beings. And McVay returns again to poetry. "If you take the central thing we've learned from Darwin, Walt Whitman does in two lines: 'I believe a leaf of grass is no less / than the journey work of the stars.' That's a huge thought."[41]

Indeed, it takes us out from our planet into the universe—an expansion of the resonant world.

The Music of the Spheres

There is geometry in the humming of the strings . . .
there is music in the spacing of the spheres.

—PYTHAGORAS

᙭

I f music is in us—and in other species—is it somehow in the world, even in the universe itself? The ancient Greeks certainly thought so: hence the famous term "music of the spheres." The mathematician and astronomer Pythagoras is thought to have originated the concept that viewed proportions in the movements of the sun, moon, and planets as a form of music. It was believed that the celestial bodies revolve around Earth in spheres. The intervals between the spheres were considered comparable to the musical intervals. The sum of all the intervals between planets was thought to equal the six whole tones of the octave. Spheres were thought to be related to the whole-number ratios of musical intervals.

Plato took up the idea. In *The Republic,* he says of the cosmos, "Upon each of its circles stood a Siren, who was carried round with its movement, uttering . . . the concords of a single scale. The idea was that each sphere emits a sound with varying pitches, like thrown objects moving through air."

We have no writings from Pythagoras himself. But as Aristotle explained it, "[The Pythagoreans] saw that the ratios of musical scales were expressible in numbers [and that] . . . all things seemed to be modeled on numbers, and numbers seemed to be the first things in the whole of nature, they supposed the elements of number to be the elements of all things, and the whole heaven to be a musical scale and a number."

Johannes Kepler used the concept of a music of the spheres twenty centuries later in his *Harmonices Mundi* (*The Harmony of the World*) in 1619; he related astrology and harmonics. He expressed the wish "to erect the magnificent edifice of the harmonic system of the musical scale . . . as God, the Creator Himself, has expressed it in harmonizing the heavenly motions." Kepler also said, "I grant you that no sounds are given forth, but I affirm . . . that the movements of the planets are modulated according to harmonic proportions."[1]

The philosophy and religions of other cultures also have theories about the cosmos and music. Some Hindu sages believed in *shabda,* or the audible life stream, which is similar to the concept of the music of the spheres. And, of course, there's the famous text from the Bible, John 1:1, "In the beginning was the Word"—which some scholars translate as: "In the beginning was sound."

Enter modern physics and astronomy as well as astronomy's subfields of astrophysics and cosmology. Cosmologists specialize in the properties of the universe as a whole. Astrophysicists focus on the physical or chemical properties of celestial bodies. Together, scientists in these fields are proving that the ancients were onto something with their ideas about a cosmic music. Astronomers are discovering that the cosmos is literally humming with the same tones that our brains translate into music—tones that may be as old as the universe itself, and that may hold the ultimate key to the power of music. And what the ancient Greeks dubbed "the music of the spheres" finds its twenty-first-century counterpart in string theory's postulation of vibration—the same vibration that creates music—as the organizing principle of the universe.

Modern scientists looking out into the universe to decipher its secrets have not necessarily been looking for a relationship to music, yet they've found it. Now we can actually listen to the sounds of the universe—at least as they're transformed by a computer into the range of human hearing.

Astronomer Mark Whittle says that we are living in the golden era of cosmology. There are so many advances, coming so quickly. As scientists come to understand the origins of the universe, they've discovered the foundations of sound and music—vibration and sound waves. The science is not always easy for a layman to comprehend, but the results truly seem miraculous.[2]

One of the great discoveries in recent decades was the mapping of the cosmic microwave background (CMB). The CMB was formed from the release of radiation after the Big Bang fourteen billion years ago. The Big Bang itself was actually silent. But as the universe expanded, the distribution of matter and energy was not totally smooth. So there were different densities in different parts of the universe, like hills and valleys that pull on matter. Mark Whittle explains that after the Big Bang: "the universe is filled with dilute gases of one form or another. It's a fairly chaotic place. The gases are subject to forces and the forces drive sound waves through them. Sound is really gases. You have a sea of gas. Gas is vibration and it forces waves."[3] Sound waves are pressure waves running through the gaseous fluid.

The CMB was first detected in 1965 by Arno Penzias and Robert Wilson of AT&T Bell Laboratories when they were trying to determine the source of the background noise in their radio antenna. But it wasn't until the 1990s that a NASA probe was able to provide an image of the CMB—frozen in time four hundred thousand years after the Big Bang (see the color insert).

The NASA WMAP (Wilkinson Microwave Anisotropy Probe) satellite shows "patchiness" in the CMB that is actually the sound waves, similar to waves on the ocean surface. And from those patches, scientists can now determine the CMB sound spectrum. By measuring the patches, they recover a sound spectrum.

Scientists can use the sound spectrum to measure the properties of the universe. As Mark Whittle says:

[The sound of the universe] can tell us about its structure and composition. That's why the CMB sound spectrum is so important to astronomers. For thousands of years, people have imagined how their world came into being, with hundreds of different versions of that story. Now we know. Far into the future, the few decades in which we now live will be recalled as a time when people first began to understand creation's true story.[4]

The first million years of the universe is called the acoustic era. That's when sound waves formed, grew, and died. That acoustic era is the equivalent of just the first day in the life of a human in terms of total life span. Over the time of that acoustic era, the gases thinned as the universe expanded. And the sound spectrum changed. The sound spectrum from the CMB shows waves created during the first four hundred thousand years or so of the universe. Think of a fossil. It's a snapshot of the sound waves created in the universe billions of years ago.

And here the story of sound and the universe gets even more remarkable. The miracle is that the early sound of the universe, which we can identify in the CMB, actually contains its overtones—just like notes played on a musical instrument. Remember that the human voice and a note played by a musical instrument have a fundamental tone but also overtones (higher pitches) of that fundamental frequency. In 2001, a group of scientists using a microwave detector at a South Pole research station, as well as a balloon-borne detector, identified two of the overtones—the first two harmonics above the main tone. Then a year later, in the Chilean Andes, astronomers got what they described as the most detailed images yet of the birth of the universe. And from those pictures, they identified a third, fourth, and perhaps the fifth and sixth overtones.[5]

These discoveries supported the theory of inflation or expansion after the Big Bang. They also led many astronomers, astrophysicists, and cosmologists to speak even more freely of the universe in musical terms. The leader of the team, astronomer Anthony Readhead, says that the Big Bang universe seems to have shaped itself using the overtone series to play what he calls "the real music of the spheres."[6] Astronomers Wayne Hu and Martin White explained the overtones that have been detected this way:

> Because inflation [of the universe] produced the density disturbances all at once in essentially the first moment of creation, the phases of all the sound waves were synchronized.[7] The result was a sound spectrum with overtones much like a musical instrument's. Consider blowing into a pipe that is open at both ends. The fundamental frequency of the sound corresponds to a wave (also called a mode of vibration) . . . The wavelength of the fundamental mode is twice the length of the pipe. But the sound also has a series of overtones corresponding to wavelengths that are integer fractions of the fundamental wavelength: one half, one third, one fourth and so on.[8]

In musical instruments, the relative strength of the harmonic overtones gives each one its unique sound. That's why a Stradivarius violin sounds different—better—than a lesser violin.

A string on a violin vibrates in a way that creates specific intervals and overtones because it's a particular length that can be divided in certain proportions. But how could a specific length of the universe be divided into certain proportions if the universe has no defined space? As scientists say, it has no "constraints." So how do we explain overtones in the sound of the universe? Here, time instead of length is the boundary.

The graph shows the relative strength of different-size patches on the microwave background, from large ones spanning a quarter of the sky, to small ones of which five could fit under the full moon. Back in the early universe, this corresponds to a range in wavelength from about 15 million light-years to 20,000 light-years. For reasons that need not concern us here, only waves shorter than 220,000 light-years are actually oscillating sound waves.[9]

As Kepler foresaw, we cannot hear the sounds of the universe in their original form because they are too low to be within the frequency range of human hearing. But if they're transposed fifty octaves higher, we can listen to the universe. Mark Whittle and some other scientists are shifting the sounds of the cosmos higher, but it's a complicated process. First, the actual sound must be calculated. Loudness, pitch, and quality must be measured. For example, the loudness of sound depends on the strength of the pressure waves. And the strength is determined by the brightness variations on the CMB. Pitch or frequency is the number of sound waves passing by our ears each second. And the sound quality depends on the relative amount of each pitch.

So what does the primordial voice of the universe sound like when transposed so we can hear it? In its rough form it has a roaring/hissing sound—not very musical. Whittle reconstructed the first four hundred thousand years of the sound spectrum so we can hear its evolution (see the color insert). He calls it a "descending scream." And that's just what it's like. The pitch drops because as the universe expands (which it continues to do, even today), the areas into which the gas is falling and bouncing out get bigger. Look at an orchestra. The bigger the instrument, the deeper the pitch.[10]

The sound also gets louder—a cosmic crescendo. Whittle

graphed the evolution of cosmic sound over the first four hundred thousand years in the form of musical notation (see the color insert).

Physicist Brian Greene, author of *The Elegant Universe*, also makes a clear analogy between the universe and music:

The mathematical relationship between the overtones in the vibrations of this primordial plasma and the relationship between a note on a piano at one octave versus another is the same relationship, the exact same relationship. It's simply a matter of how quickly the vibration is taking place. So from that perspective it really is the same as the musical relationships that distinguish middle C from high C. In a way it is totally remarkable. The way in which a single idea that can move us in a concert hall is at work in the cosmos. But then when you take a step back and you realize that it's all a matter of the same underlying phenomena, vibration, and vibration is so apparent in the universe, that you see the unifying thread. That's what's going on.[11]

Mark Whittle points out that the poet Dryden had it pretty right:

From Harmony, from heavenly harmony,
This universal frame began:
When nature underneath a heap
Of jarring atoms lay,
And could not heave her head,
The tuneful voice was heard from high,

"Arise, ye more than dead!"
Then cold, and hot, and moist, and dry,
In order to their stations leap,
And Music's power obey.[12]

Close analysis of the early sounds of the universe is yielding even more interesting information. That raw sound we can hear when it's shifted fifty octaves to suit our ears is just the tip of the iceberg. The sound spectrum of a flute, say, contains narrow harmonics. But the cosmic sound contains what are called broad harmonics (see the color insert). That is, the distance between the fundamental and harmonic overtones is broad. As Mark Whittle suggests, imagine pushing down two octaves' worth of keys on the piano. It doesn't sound too pretty; the fundamental note of the universe is also wide.[13]

In musical terms, what are the harmonics, or chords, of the early universe? It's fascinating to learn that the primary interval—the bottom two notes—are a Major third that evolves to a minor third. Then there's another evolution to a full chord that includes both a Major third and a minor third. A violin or a flute has what are called perfect harmonics because they're equally spaced. A drum or cymbals have more complicated harmonics. They don't have a simple relationship and one generally doesn't hear a specific tone in the sound. The universe is closer to a violin or a flute, though not quite the same.

The cosmic tones actually contain a missing fundamental—like the one in music. Our brain "hears" it even if we consciously don't. For example, if part of a Major triad (C, E, G) is played on the piano missing the C, our brain fills it in. The missing fundamental even comes into play when we use the telephone. The phone doesn't accurately transmit all the frequencies of a person's voice. Yet our brain "imagines" the missing tones and we recognize the voice.

And the story of sound in the universe continues. Sound waves played a key role in the creation of the first stars. As time passed, the sound waves grew with expansion; the sound became louder and the pitch dropped. It became more of a hiss as gas fell into dark matter clumps (assisted by dark matter). This is a simplification. The details belong to the scientists! At any rate, this collapsing matter became the first stars, which in turn merged into star clusters and then into galaxies.

As they map the evolution of the universe, scientists are also going back to those first moments after the Big Bang—when there was silence. What actually caused the first unevenness in gas density that created sound waves? The answer is not yet really known. It's believed that the so-called patchiness that the CMB shows is all due to quantum fluctuations that are amplified by early inflation of the universe—a theory first proposed in the 1980s. So before those quantum fluctuations moved, they were already in place, holding the spectrum of pure noise.

Mark Whittle imagines the seeds of cosmic sound like this:

Although all is deathly quiet, there is present throughout the entire Universe an exceedingly rich *latent* sound ready to burst forth, simply waiting for gravity's order to arrive. In a sense, space was filled with a silent sound, a silence so rich that within it all future sounds were already present. If we could somehow cheat time, and unlock all this sound at once, what would it sound like?

What a bold aim—to render audible this opening silence, pristine and raw, unaltered by gravity or time—the ultimate source of all that is to come. Surely, it will be an enthralling sound?[14]

When I read this, I think of all the musicians who talk about the "silence between the notes" as being such a crucial part of music. DBR, the cross-genre violinist, told me, "You know it's not so much the sound of the violin; it's the silence thereafter. That's the moment when in some ways you hear what was just said."[15] The composer Claude Debussy said, "Music is the silence between the notes."

Daniel Barenboim, the renowned pianist and conductor, observed about the nature of sound:

Sound has several very interesting aspects that I think worth observing. One is its duration; there is a connection between sound and time. But before that there is a connection between sound and silence. The duration of sound and its relation to silence is a very objective thing. If I sing a note or whistle a note, when I have no more air the note goes. Where does it go? Into the silence again. Sound has a relationship with silence, not unlike the law of gravity. In order to lift a certain object from the ground, we have to use energy, and then to maintain it at that level we have to keep on adding energy; otherwise the object falls to the ground. It's exactly the same thing with the sound. We need a certain amount of energy to produce the sound. But then to sustain it, we have to give more energy; otherwise it goes and it dies in silence. Therefore sound is absolutely inextricably connected to time. And I think this is what gives it its really tragic element, even more so when it becomes music—the fact that the sound can die, the fact that every note is a lifetime for itself.[16]

A recent scientific study is showing why silence is so meaningful in music. Elizabeth Margulis, a researcher at the University of Arkansas, showed that people respond differently to pauses in music depending on the music around the pause. They perceived various degrees of changes in both the duration and the amount of tension in the silence. Also, Margulis found that some listeners reported hearing differences in what they perceived as the *meter* of the silence. They actually heard a rhythm in the silence. The most rhythmic silence in Margulis's study was in an excerpt from Beethoven's Hammerklavier Sonata after a pattern of strong and then soft beats had been established. Listeners then supplied their own answering pulse during the pause in response to the pattern. Margulis writes that "impressions of the music that preceded the silence seep into the gap, as do expectations of what may follow."[17]

Silence is part of music just as it is part of cosmic sound.

Scientists find more relationships between music and the universe. An analogy between music and quantum field theory is what drew physicist Stephon Alexander to the field. He plays the saxophone. Here's how he tells the story:

There was a time actually in grad school when I didn't know that I wanted to become a physicist. I was just like, what am

I doing? I'm wasting my time here. I'm going to be sitting behind a desk doing this stuff? Maybe I should get out into the world and actually help humanity in some way. And then, actually the day I decided that I was going to leave, I noticed on the desk a book called *Quantum Field Theory*, and I opened the book and it starts off: "Quantum field theory is analogous to a picture of matter; like a gigantic orchestra, the vibration of the field gives rise to the different forms of matter." So it's the underlying paradigm of matter and energy vibrating in this gigantic orchestra and the appearance of matter, or substance, in all these things are just really this orchestra's field, vibrating. And immediately I said to myself, wow, like you mean, physics is no different in this way than music, meaning that, if I have an orchestra or a band, there are things going on individually between the players. But then there's this overall effect of the whole, and the harmony that's generated with the whole. And so, that view of physics actually made me realize I should continue on.[18]

Brian Greene is not surprised that scientists see these connections with music and speak of scientific phenomena in musical terms.

There are a great many metaphors that scientists love to use in describing their work and their breakthroughs. Musical metaphors stand in a class by themselves because it's not just a metaphor, because the musical idea actually can be embodied in equations and those equations are tightly akin to the actual equations that we use in our work. So musical metaphors are very satisfying because they're not just vague ideas that are used to help the nonscientist understand what the scientist is doing, it's a metaphor that takes you very close to the true nature of the scientific work.[19]

Stephon Alexander believes "there is a deep connection between geometry and music." He's working on a study to see if there's more than just an analogous relationship between music and the cosmos but "a relationship at the higher levels of organized sound." He's looking at geometries common in physics that he thinks are also found in classical music. As a musician, he's found a way to visualize finger patterns on the saxophone in geometrical patterns.[20]

The universe is truly an ocean of sound; it's not just metaphor and hypothesis. The Pythagoreans were wrong about the planets revolving around the earth in spheres that create sound, but the planets *do* make sound waves as they move and their gravitational field pulls. NASA conducted experiments using the Voyager space probes to pick up the electromagnetic vibrations of planets and record them within the human hearing range of twenty to twenty thousand cycles per second. The sounds are weird and wonderful. Even the earth has a hum. Every object has a natural frequency at which to vibrate.

Astrophysicist Gregory Laughlin at the University of California has created software that converts mathematical models of planetary movement into sounds. The planets orbit stars causing the star to move; Laughlin plots the movement as an audible waveform.[21]

There are many acoustic objects in the cosmos. The sun has many harmonics. Helioseismologists use computer-generated graphics to show the pattern of solar acoustic oscillation—that is, sound waves.

And within the last decade or so, scientists have actually been able to pick up and identify the pitches of other objects in the universe. A recent study by Adam Burrows at the University of Arizona indicates that sound waves actually cause the final collapse of dying stars. They start to vibrate as they die, creating sound waves that have audible frequencies in the range of 200 to 400 hertz—around middle C. The energy of the sound waves may provide the final blow.[22] And Brian Greene told me that neutron stars rotating around each other have vibrations that cause gravitational waves—not in air

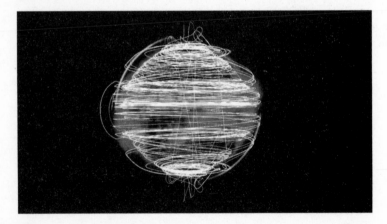

FIGURE 5 Solar acoustic (pressure) waves. CREDIT: NASA

but in space and time. These waves can be translated into sound. People have done those simulations, and we can hear the stars.

Even black holes sing. Dr. Andrew Fabian, an x-ray astronomer at the Institute of Astronomy at Cambridge University in England, headed the international team that first heard the sound of a black hole. In 2003, they used NASA's Chandra X-ray Observatory to detect the black hole's "notes" as ripples of luminosity in the Perseus cluster of galaxies. Gas falling into a black hole develops chaotic behavior that creates vibration. The "notes" are pressure waves rolling through a gas that fills the galaxy. These waves are thirty thousand light-years across with a period of oscillation of ten million years! The lowest notes that humans can hear have a period of about one twentieth of a second. Fabian called this black hole "note" "the lowest note in the universe." And he specified its frequency as a B-flat—fifty-seven octaves below middle C, way outside the human hearing range.[23] Some scientists question whether one can specify such a cosmic note so precisely. But there's no doubt it's a low one!

The following year another group of scientists heard another black hole. This one was spreading out from the center of a galaxy called the M87. These sound waves are an octave higher than the ones from the Perseus black hole and a little less pure. Dr. William Forman of the Harvard-Smithsonian Center for Astrophysics was quoted as saying, "If one could hear the sound, it would be more like the cannons in the '1812 Overture' than the pure tone of a musical instrument.[24]

* * *

The musical metaphors in the universe take on another dimension—pun intended—with string theory. Brian Greene, a leading expert in that field, summarizes the idea:

String theory is an approach to describing the fundamental constituents of matter. So we know about molecules and atoms and subatomic particles. String theory goes a little further and says inside of all particles is a little tiny string that vibrates, sort of like the string on a violin would vibrate, and the equations that we use to describe the vibrations of these little tiny strings at the heart of matter are very close in structure to the equation that we'd use to describe the motion of a string on a violin. An electron might be a string vibrating in one pattern. You can call it a middle C if you want the musical analogy. A quark would be a string vibrating in a different pattern, like an A. So the difference between one particle and another is simply the note that its string is playing. So in a sense, what we're saying is that . . . at the heart of matter is music. At the heart of matter are vibrating filaments, vibrating through their sound, matter and energy, maybe even space and time into existence. So there's a real fundamental way in which musical metaphors really brush right up against cutting-edge ideas in physics.[25]

A few years ago, Greene created a program with the Emerson String Quartet. The program, called "Strings and Strings," brought the musical metaphors of mathematics and physics to life.

* * *

Just as many musicians have incorporated birdsong into their works over the centuries, the new science of cosmic sound is inspiring composers today. The Kronos string quartet performs a multimedia production, Sun Rings, that's based on sounds of space collected by University of Iowa professor Don Gurnett.[26] Grateful Dead percussionist Mickey Hart is also captivated by cosmic sound. He's made a film, *Rhythms of the Universe*, in collaboration with Nobel Prize–winning physicist George Smoot III. Hart wanted to incorporate sounds from the cosmos into his compositions. He says, "Every story needs a beginning. In my case as a rhythmist, I wanted to go back to beat one, the creation of time and space, and that would of course be the Big Bang."[27]

For the sound track of Hart's film, the light waves of exploding supernovas were translated into sound. Berkeley National Laboratory computer scientist Keith Jackson, who's also a musician, converted the electromagnetic data from the light waves by slowing down the frequency and elongating or "stretching" it into audio form. It sounds like a deep rumble— rather like an earthquake. Mickey Hart then took these sounds and used them to create music.[28]

Hart is convinced of the connection between music, the cosmos, and human life. He says, "It comes down to the fact that it's vibration and fundamental harmonics that causes it all to be linked together. I wanted to hear what the universe sounded like and I wanted to interact with it and have a conversation with it because those sound waves are like our ancestors; they are where we came from."[29] Hart intuits that our biology is an echo of the cosmos. It's likely we are entrained to the larger universal rhythm that surrounds us. We are our universe. "It's where it all came from," Hart says. "George [Smoot] sees it as the face of God. I see it as the sound of God."[30]

It's a big idea—and one that scientists are also considering. Astronomer Mark Whittle, for example, proposes that sound *does* connect humans to the cosmos. He reminds us of the Darwinian idea that all organisms adapt to the environment to survive. So we can see light, see the stars of the universe, Whittle continues, because sight is a survival mechanism. So why should it surprise us, he asks, that when we can hear the sounds of the cosmos with their overtones, there's recognition? We shouldn't be surprised, he continues, because organisms adapt to sound just as they do to light. Perhaps we evolved to hear the sounds of the universe. Whittle says, "Just as light brings intonation to the eyes, sound brings intonation to the ears. We are evolving in the cosmos and some of its qualities are going to be part of who we are."[31]

But is it possible that when we see connections between ourselves, our earthly world, our music, and the universe that we're just imposing our perspective on the cosmos? Whittle believes that "what we see and what we hear are not actually the external world, but they're reconstructions that our brain makes of that external world." He says, "What we experience as the external world is actually inside our heads. So there must be a correspondence between the internal and external worlds."[32]

It's a huge idea in the quest to solve the riddle of music's meaning in the natural world that surrounds us. Stephon Alexander is also thinking of a convergence between our universe and our selves:

When we go into the fundamental questions that physics is really asking, questions of how is matter really created, and we look back at the correlation of how is the universe music, we can't help to wonder how interesting would it be, if the mystery as to why we like music, or why there's something universal about music and harmony across cultures—and why matter is manifested, in our universe, in this harmonious picture, as physicists describe, might have a similar route.[33]

The story of the universe and music is especially one that seems only to add to the awe and mystery of both scientific and artistic discovery. I've been reminded of a quote from the great physicist Richard Feynman:

I have a friend who's an artist, and he sometimes takes a view which I don't agree with. He'll hold up a flower and say, "Look how beautiful it is," and I'll agree. But then he'll say, "I, as an artist, can see how beautiful a flower is. But you, as a scientist, take it all apart and it becomes dull." There are all kinds of interesting questions that come from a knowledge of science, which only adds to the excitement and mystery and awe of a flower. It only adds. I don't understand how it subtracts.[34]

Plato believed that the universe is controlled by mathematical and scientific law. Yet he was also a mystic. Dr. Jay Kenney, who wrote a recent paper about musical codes in Plato's writings, notes that the Greek saw beauty in his vision of music as mathematical and mathematics as musical. He saw this conjunction as divine.[35] The Hindu sages who saw the music of the spheres as connected to all life thought Pythagoras was one of them.

It's a remarkable concept that music is at the heart of the universe. Or as Louis Armstrong once put it, "What we play is life." Science, beauty—and biology—meet through music. I'm reminded of my father's paper written decades ago, theorizing that music echoes our bodies. Today's science is leading us to wonder if sound and music are not the echo of everything.

PART IV

Music RX

CHAPTER 11

Pain, Pills—or Music?

A person does not hear sound only through the ears;
He hears sound through every pore of his body,
It permeates the entire being . . .
In that way the physical body recuperates
and becomes charged with new magnetism.

—HAZRAT INAYAT KHAN

To see tears come to the eyes of a neuroscientist as music enables a stroke patient to speak is to witness a moment filled with promise. Science is opening doors to medical applications of music that were unimaginable a decade or so ago. Play music and Parkinson's disease patients walk, stroke victims speak, the aging remember, and the heartbeats of premature infants stabilize. Scientists predict a future in which music will routinely be used as a prescription, when it will alter our genetic makeup, treat immune system disorders, and alter brain function in neurologically disabled and aging patients.

Our ancestors believed in the use of music for healing. And today, many cultures around the world maintain these ancient traditions. There are numerous medicine men and shamans whose rituals include musical components. Ghanaian healers use belief systems that incorporate music to ease pain. Ethiopian church musicians are also healers. The story of Ethiopia's Saint Yared is a classic myth symbolizing the medicinal powers of music. Yared sang to the emperor, and when the emperor's spear pierced Yared's foot, Yared felt no pain. The Bible, too, describes David playing his harp to ease King Saul's physical and mental suffering. Ethnomusicologist Kay Shelemay is pleased to point out that "now people in Western biomedicine are looking at what's happening in other cultures." Today, science is transforming the idea of music as medicine from myth and guesswork to treatments with proven effect.

In modern hospitals, music is frequently used to ease pain and reduce the amount of anesthesia required during surgery. In England, patients who listened to classical music while undergoing local anesthesia recovered more quickly and reported fewer complications. In Canada, patients exposed to fifteen minutes of soothing music needed half the sedatives and anesthetic drugs compared to other patients. In Poland, patients with chronic severe headaches experienced reduced need for medication after they listened to concert music for six months. At UMass Memorial Health Care, harp music is often prescribed in place of tranquilizers for cancer patients. In Texas, women needed less anesthesia during childbirth when listening to music. At the Cleveland Clinic, studies show that when surgical patients listened to recorded music, it decreased their post-surgical pain fourfold. Live-music therapy decreased anxiety

56.73 percent for chemotherapy patients, while those without the therapy saw an increase in anxiety of 11 percent. And the list could go on.

Singer Carly Simon has founded a music-therapy program with the Berklee College of Music in Boston. She says, "The way music can be used as a healing tool is remarkable. I will sing while holding the hands of people who are about to go under anesthesia, sometimes I sing 'I Haven't Got Time for the Pain,' as doctors are counting down from 17, and the look of peace I can see wash over them really proves to me the power of music to tap into the core of the human psyche."[1]

Dr. Claudius Conrad, a surgical resident at Harvard Medical School who trained as a classical pianist growing up in Europe, had no doubt that music aids in reducing blood pressure, steadies heart rate, eases stress, and helps patients heal. But he wanted to investigate the medical processes behind the effect of music and gather data because only data will persuade insurance companies to start reimbursing for music therapy. In 2007 he did a study on critically ill intubated patients in the intensive care unit. The patients, while off sedation, listened to a one-hour session of slow movements from Mozart's piano sonatas. The study measured a set of stress hormones, cytokines, and physiological parameters such as heart rate and blood pressure before and after the music sessions. The study showed that compared to controls the music significantly reduced the amount of sedative drugs necessary to reach comparable levels of sedation.

Moreover, Dr. Conrad got one result he didn't expect. He thought that one of the hormones that would probably show lower levels with relaxation would be the growth hormone.

But the patients who heard the music showed *increased* levels of growth hormone along with reduced levels of the stress hormones interleukin-6 and epinephrine.[2] Dr. Conrad titled the paper he wrote about this study "Overture for Growth Hormone: Requiem for Interleukin-6?" What actually happens, the study revealed, is that white blood cells have a receptor on the surface that's called a growth hormone receptor. When the growth hormone binds to that receptor, less interleukin-6—a key stress hormone—is secreted from those cells. He suggests that music may have healing and sedative effects because of a neurohormonal pathway. Conrad says the study "raised some wonderful new possibilities about the physiology of healing. And of course it has a nice sort of metaphorical ring. We used to talk about the neuroendocrine system being a sort of neuronal orchestra conductor directing the immune system. Here we have music stimulating this conductor to get the healing process started."[3]

The study also raised new questions. It's not yet clear exactly what the jump in growth hormone levels means. And it's not known if only the music of Mozart has such an effect.

Conrad's doctoral dissertation examined why and how Mozart's music seemed to ease the pain of intensive-care patients. He analyzed the structure of the music, pointing to short repeated phrases with subtle variations in the pattern—a combination of soothing melody and stimulating complexity. He speculates that Mozart himself suffered from near-constant illness. Perhaps he wrote the music to heal himself.

At the moment, Conrad and other doctors who use music for postsurgical healing usually choose classical recordings. According to a study by researchers at Gagnon Cardiovascular Institute in New Jersey, the vibrations of stringed instruments are able to "mesh" with the energy of the heart, small intestine, pericardium, and thyroid and adrenal glands.⁴ The harp, of course, has lots of strings. So perhaps that's why it's been used so much in music therapy.

In his quest to prove the effect of music therapy with hard data, Conrad is also looking at ways to standardize protocols to use music to reduce the need for narcotics during surgical recovery. It's known that a reduction in sedative drugs leads to better survival rates.

Music therapists have long known intuitively and anecdotally that their techniques can ease stress and lower heart rate. But the public perception of music therapy has often been that it *is* based on mere intuition and guesswork. That perception— certainly regarding certified music therapists—is rapidly changing because the therapy is increasingly based on hard scientific evidence and research studies.

At New York City's Beth Israel Medical Center, music therapist Carol Lowey works with premature infants in the neonatal intensive care unit—the NICU. As she uses her fingers to rhythmically play a wooden Gato box, an instrument similar to a drum, the infant's heart rate slows and steadies. The idea is to entrain to the baby's heart rate. She says, "The fetus hears the mother's heart beat twenty-six million times before the baby is born. So, with the Gato box, we can actually re-create heart sounds, and that's been very important for the babies."

She also uses an instrument called an ocean disc that mimics the sound inside the womb. Again, Lowey is entraining to the baby's own rhythm of heartbeat and breath. Then the heart rate slows as the infant settles.

The therapists also sing to the infants, using certain intervals. Lowey explained that they use consonant intervals, usually Major and minor thirds.

The Beth Israel music-therapy department is collecting data from eight NICUs to study effects on heart rate and respiratory rate from music therapy. One completed study compared the use of medication (chloral hydrate) to music and found that live-music therapy—as opposed to recorded music—was more successful in putting the babies to sleep.[5]

Like many other hospitals, Beth Israel also uses music to regulate the heart and respiratory rates of adult cardiac patients. And their methods promise to become increasingly sophisticated as scientists come to understand more details about how music works on the body's physiological system.

At the Cleveland Clinic, neurologist Dr. Kamal Chemali studies how the central autonomic network gives orders to the body, regulating the sympathetic and parasympathetic nervous systems, complementary systems for managing stress. The parasympathetic system essentially says "rest" or put the brakes on; whereas the sympathetic system accelerates everything and is associated with the fight-or-flight response. Chemali has tested different types of music in order to specify the effects of changes in tempo and pitch—and the silence in between sections or movements. Fast tempos did increase heart rate, while slow tempos resulted in a decrease. But interestingly, a Schubert lullaby produced a decrease in parasympathetic tone and an increase in sympathetic tone. Since the sympathetic nervous system is for arousal, clearly there was still arousal even with a soothing melody. Chemali cautions that this indicates that really arousing music—like heavy metal—could be dangerous for people with heart problems. Another interesting result of his study was that during the pauses, the silences, all the parasympathetic markers went down—even lower than the baseline level. Perhaps it's in those silences that music invokes deep rest and relaxation.[6]

Damir Janigro, director of cerebrovascular research at the Cleveland Clinic, has reported the discovery of an area deep inside the brain that no one even knew was involved in the processing of music. In a study, Janigro recorded neuronal activity from Parkinson's disease patients who must be awake when undergoing brain surgery. This deep-brain stimulation surgery is used to treat movement disorders. While the patient was on the table, Janigro and his team were able to see the response of deep-brain structures like the thalamus and subthalamic nuclei to music. They chose specific, specially composed music for the experiment to mimic either melodic or rhythmic pieces. They purposely chose appropriate music unfamiliar to the patients because they didn't want musical memory or associations to interfere. The results of the experiment showed that melodic music decreased the frequency of neuronal firing. The meaning of this new finding is still not clear, though it may be consistent with reduction of stress. But the ability to record the activity of single neuronal cells is a technique that is offering a new ability to "crack the Morse code of music and the brain," Janigro said. It offers the potential to greatly refine future applications of music therapy. For example, it could mean that music may one day be widely used in operating rooms to achieve specific effects on patient anxiety during surgery.[7]

Some oncologists are integrating sound and music therapy

into their practices, using a variety of methods. Dr. Mitchell Gaynor, an oncologist in New York City, has been using music and sound for years. When patients come to Dr. Gaynor, who is the director of Medical Oncology and Integrative Medicine at the Strang Cancer Prevention Center, they get the standard medical treatment—discussion of chemotherapy and other options, prognosis, etc. Then they are also given an introductory session of sound meditation. Dr. Gaynor says that his patients tell him that on this most stressful day of their lives, they have never felt more relaxed. Gaynor uses Tibetan singing bowls. His work with sound began when a patient, a Tibetan monk, gave him a bowl as a gift. Gaynor was struck by the tones and the overtones. He could both hear and feel the vibrations. He started using sound therapy and says he saw patients achieve remarkable relaxation and inner peace. In addition to the bowls, Gaynor finds chanting helpful. The clinical evidence of stress reduction through sound therapy is clear to him. But he also points to the scientific literature showing that sound can affect many aspects of the body. Studies show the interleuken-1 level, an index of the immune system, goes up after sound meditation. And immunoglobulin levels in the blood are increased.[8]

There's research in the field of neurocardiology on the link between the heart and the brain. Heart rate variability (HRV) shows how the heart rate changes. And the HRV is high when we're stressed, lower when we listen to peaceful music. The interesting part is that studies show the brain waves also change to ones associated with relaxation states. The magnetic field of the heart seems to be affecting the brain.[9]

Stress, of course, is a problem that affects not only patients but the whole population. U.S. doctor visits involve stress-related complaints 60 to 90 percent of the time. A fledgling scientific field, called psychoneuroimmunology, has emerged recently and focuses on the interaction between our thoughts, feelings, and beliefs and the nervous, immune, and endocrine systems. The immune system and the nervous system are wired together and interact in creating biological changes.

The effect of music on the immune system has been the chief focus for several years at the Mind-Body Wellness Center in Meadville, Pennsylvania. Dr. Barry Bittman, neurologist and director of the center, is also at the forefront of efforts to provide hard data for music's therapeutic effects. Bittman has done research showing that group music making reduces stress in nursing students and long-term care workers.[10]

Over the last decade, his research has entered new territory. In 2001, Bittman published a paper outlining results from a study on the effects of group drumming—recreational music making—on the immune system.[11] At that time, cortisol and other stress hormones were the markers used by Dr. Bittman's team and other researchers. The results were complex. But the data seemed to indicate that the activity enhanced the immune system. Still—there was clearly a need for more study. One group was submitted to stress through intensive drumming and yet their cortisol levels dropped. Bittman says cortisol is not tied to all stress pathways; it's a nonspecific indicator of stress.[12]

Bittman moved on to genetics as a way to find markers of stress and to study the effects of recreational music making. For his first study, the research team included scientists from the Loma Linda University School of Medicine and Applied

Biosystems, developer of the technology that led to successful mapping of the human genome in 2000. Subjects were first asked to work on a frustrating puzzle exercise. Then they were divided into three groups. The first continued the stressful puzzle exercise. The second could relax and read newspapers or magazines. The third engaged in group music making. Then the groups' blood was sampled for forty-five known genomic markers—molecular switches that turn on biological responses associated with health problems ranging from heart disease to cancer. Bittman calls the results "groundbreaking." The research showed that the stress reduction was greater for the subjects who played musical instruments than for those who read. More than three times as many genomic markers for stress were reversed in the music group compared to the other. And that was with people with little or no musical training, just learning to play an instrument.

To reduce these beginners' fears of making mistakes, Bittman used a specially designed beginner's system with an electronic keyboard. It's not known how much of the response was due to the music per se and how much to participation in a group activity.[13] But Bittman notes that "the genome gives a view of molecular structures in real time. For the first time, we have a view of exactly what's happening in real time on a molecular level." It's significant, he says, that this first study showed that the stress response was not uniform among all the subjects. The genome markers showed that different people respond in different ways to the same stress inducers. In terms of the response to music, this is important because each person may respond to a given piece of music differently. Bittman says, "This makes the music response complicated. But that's what we need—individual responses. We need specificity." He believes that there's too much generalization in the music-science field—like saying all music is relaxing. Bittman wants music medicine to be accurate and individualized when necessary.[14]

Bittman says his group is doing the only genomic work focused on the effect of music. "What we're doing biologically and socially will move music research into the future," he says. "Analyzing the human genome enables us to precisely detect the biological switches that literally turn on the entire cascade leading to all other effects. It's really about getting close to the source of the biological response, and tracking the overall process on the molecular level."

Bittman says of music science: "We have to admit we're at the embryonic stage. Technology is just catching up with the questions."[15] But clearly, the understanding of music's healing potential has moved far beyond the stage of merely playing the harp at the bedside of sick and dying patients—helpful as that may be.

Many of the most significant developments regarding music and medicine are driven by the new understanding of the interaction between music and the brain. It truly is powerful and very moving to see music spark speech in a stroke patient, movement in a person with Parkinson's disease, and musical memory in an Alzheimer's patient. There's a term for the therapeutic methods that have grown out of the neuroscience research regarding music: neurologic music therapy. This is what's being used at Beth Abraham Hospital's Institute for Music and Neurologic Function in New York City to treat stroke patients.

The institute is headed by a pioneer in music therapy, Dr. Concetta Tomaino, who cofounded it with Dr. Oliver Sacks. In one room, a patient who has had a stroke, "Cheryl," was having a music-therapy session, singing words and phrases she had trouble speaking. Then she was tested with cards showing common objects like a dress or a lipstick to record her improvement. Before music therapy, her repetition score was in the seventies. Now it's in the nineties on an immediate task. Repetition is important in speech because it allows the patient to express herself fluently. Ultimately, the goal is to use music to improve spontaneous language—not just specific individual tasks.

When I met Cheryl she had also demonstrated a 15 percent improvement in her word-finding score. She has aphasia resulting from a stroke to the left side of the brain. People with aphasia know the words, but can't get them out. The speech therapist has become a big supporter of music therapy and she uses it with all her aphasia patients. The repetition of the melody line helps, as does the rhythm of the music. And the patient relaxes, reducing stress if there's a mistake. But, as Tomaino points out, it's the new understanding of the brain that makes music such a promising therapy for neurologic disorders.[16]

In the past, some people have intuited that potential. The singer Carly Simon had a stammer as a child. She remembers that her mother told her, "Don't speak it, sing it." And that's what she did, eliminating the stammer.[17]

Where before there was only guesswork, science has shown the apparent relationship between music and language networks in the brain. Tomaino says, "Music accesses the networks in the brain in a complementary fashion or differently than the function that the person has lost. And what I mean by that is that we can stimulate the timing mechanisms; we can stimulate the word-finding ability; we can stimulate recognition memory and even short-term memory function. Through using music in a specific way, that makes available to the patients function in the brain that's still there, but maybe they can't do independently because of the inhibition that has taken place due to their brain injury."

Tomaino and her colleagues use familiar songs to stimulate word-retrieval abilities. Then as the person improves, they also introduce a form of a technique called melodic intonation therapy (MIT).

Neurologist Gottfried Schlaug, in Boston, is an expert in a similar method designed specifically to use music making/singing to stimulate the brain to compensate for damaged areas. Schlaug uses MIT to help the communication skills of aphasia patients who've lost the ability to speak due to a stroke but still can understand speech. He used it to work with a young mother, "K," only in her thirties. She wanted to at least be able to communicate with her daughter. Like other aphasics, she understood words but could not speak. Melodic intonation therapy actually works only if the patient understands the words.

It's important to note that reports describing patients' ability to sing words and phrases they cannot speak have been reported in scientific literature for more than one hundred years—for instance, stroke patients who could get the words out if they hum. But there wasn't much research; most of the evidence was anecdotal. And the bedside observation had not been turned into a therapy protocol. Then in 1973 a group in Boston developed MIT. The version that Schlaug is using is more advanced than the original method. The patient who

wants to say, "How are you today?" is prompted by a therapist
to say that in a melodic phrase—singing it, in fact. Schlaug
explains that "the melodic intonation seems to engage areas in
the right side of the brain, particularly in the right temporal
and parietal lobe. And this is already known from normal subjects. If I would ask either a nonmusician or a musician to process melodic contour, or to pay particular attention to a melody,
or do a contour of a musical piece, I would see that there's more
activity on the right side of the brain. So the right side of the
brain seems to be better equipped in integrating over time and
in recognizing the overall structure, the contour, or the melody
of a piece. So, by using melodic intonation, we seem to be able
to engage more the right side of the brain."[18]

Both sides of the brain may have the ability to support vocal
production. The left side can certainly do this without the right.
And scientists believe the right may be able to do this as well
without large portions of the left. We also know that many parts
of the brain can adapt and change with intense and long-term
training. So the right side of the brain could well compensate
for the damaged left side when patients show improvement
with melodic intonation therapy. And there's a second component to MIT. The patient taps with the left hand at the rate that
syllables are reproduced by the patient and the therapist. This
engages the sensory motor network on the right side of the
brain, which is important for connecting sounds to articulatory
actions. At the end of her therapy session, the young mother, K,
clearly intoned, "Wait for me." Now she had the tools to caution
her toddler daughter on the street.

Melodic intonation therapy is a long process, Schlaug
cautions: "The real trick of the therapy is to actually get patients

back to speaking again through a form of singing. This is a very intense process that requires many, many therapy sessions, a lot of practice from the patients, but it can be achieved after this high-intensity intervention. And after one gets a patient back to speaking again, if it is only single words or short phrases, then there are many other opportunities for that patient to engage in other therapies that can now improve word length, sentence length, or sentence structures, et cetera."

Schlaug hopes that melodic intonation therapy will become more widely used to help patients who are receiving no other treatment as well as those receiving interventions that could be enhanced by the addition of MIT.

A trained organist and singer, Schlaug is very moved when he watches melodic intonation therapy at work: "The satisfying part about this is that I can use . . . my musical background and my musical skill and apply that to help my patients. So that is very gratifying, actually, and it brings me to tears, you know, to see that people and patients who have not been able to speak at all now are actually able to say words, simple sentences, to express their most basic needs."[19]

There's now evidence that melodic intonation and other therapies using music to facilitate speech in patients with neurologic disorders produce results. But they take time—months of sessions that insurance does not cover. The therapists and scientists working in this field are hoping to change that by making an irrefutable case that music works.

Neuroscientist Robert Zatorre finds it hard to underestimate the possible future therapies that would take advantage of the brain's plasticity, its ability to change and adapt to a disability. He says, "We need to understand the how and why of these effects. Because if we can figure out how one part of the brain is able to stand in for another part, the implications of that are enormous. It means that if we knew how that happened, we could conceivably take someone who's had, let's say, a stroke where one part of the brain is damaged and figure out a way to retrain another area to take over that function." Because the brain is "plastic," because it can change even late in adulthood, neuroscientist Zatorre sees great possibilities for using music to stem the aging process. He calls the vision of what music can do in the future "the stuff of science fiction" that's now, shockingly, within reach.[20]

Music is already being used clinically to help patients with other neurologic disorders. Just as music and speech pathways seem to overlap in the brain, so do the auditory and motor pathways. Music has a dramatic effect on people with the degenerative neurologic disorder Parkinson's disease. Parkinson's patients freeze and have trouble starting to move. Michael Thaut, director of the Center for Biomedical Research at Colorado State University, is a pioneer in the use of music for people with movement disorders, including Parkinson's. Thaut has shown how he helps patients improve the velocity and stride of their gait by practicing movements in time to rhythmic music. He's done numerous clinical studies on the connection between rhythmicity—the state of being rhythmic or responding rhythmically—and brain function. The neuroscience research formed the foundation for using music in movement rehabilitation by showing that the motor and auditory systems are connected on many levels—cortical, subcortical, and spinal. We know now, for example, that sound can arouse and excite spinal motor neurons. And a dance tune in 2/4 meter can entrain the timing of muscle-activation patterns, as measured by electro-myography (EMG). This facilitates movement in rhythmic hop-ping.[21] Thaut points out that "the study of the neurobiology of rhythm was also the first area in which new research insights helped to establish a new role for music in rehabilitation, moving from a more social science and cultural value driven approach that emphasized 'well-being' and 'relationship building' to a neuroscience-based understanding of music to retrain and re-educate the injured brain."[22]

Thaut first noticed the effect of rhythmic cueing on arm movements. Then he and his team found improvement in stride symmetry and gait. His group developed protocols for rhyth-mic auditory stimulation (RAS) as a gait-training technique. It's now standard in neurologic music therapy. The technique uses an auditory cue—a rhythm—to produce entrainment to that rhythm, a "sensory timer" that locks in the auditory-motor system. It's also used with stroke patients.[23]

Some therapists are trying the technique on spinal cord pa-tients to see if music can activate central neuron generators. So far, results show that some patients entrain but still struggle to match the beat. Certainly, there's the prospect of more re-search into what could be an exciting application.

The rhythmic cueing in Thaut's method carries the person along as he or she is walking to the music. Some Parkinson's patients spontaneously use music, even if they haven't had for-mal therapy.

Pamela Quinn, a dancer who has Parkinson's disease, cer-tainly believes that the rhythmic structure of music is essential in supporting movement. Quinn was forty-two years old and dancing professionally when she was diagnosed. She watched as her hands began to flutter, and then it became difficult to walk across a room. For someone whose life and identity was based on movement, it was devastating. But music and dance turned out to play a very important part in her therapy. She realized that when her body began to work in an uncoordinated way, music helped put her back on track. Before she began to take medicine, music *was* her medicine. She says, "Fitting my gait into an even tempo, the speed of which matched the length of my stride, helped pull everything together." As her disease progresses and she does need medication, music helps her get through the difficult times between doses. Pamela Quinn is convinced of the value of music and movement in managing Parkinson's. She says, "I believe music is good both for the immediate moment and for the long term because I think that the more often you can reinforce normal moving patterns, the slower the disease progresses."[24]

Quinn acknowledges that this is her intuitive feeling—not science. But the science does support the idea that the repetitive rhythmic patterns of music can strengthen the brain networks used in movement. She prefers using an iPod with headphones rather than speakers: "I found that being surrounded by music, by having the music right in my ears, it was more effective than coming from a speaker. I was surrounded by sound. I was inside it." She also found that the effects were stronger when she listened to music she liked. At first she had four selections—a march, a rock song, Mozart, and Bach. But eventually her repertoire expanded.

She became so convinced that music could help others with Parkinson's disease that she developed a program called

Movement Lab to teach her techniques to other people with Parkinson's. She took the idea to an arts advocacy group for people with Parkinson's that holds classes at the Mark Morris Dance Center in Brooklyn, where she now teaches classes. She also teaches at the New York College of Osteopathic Medicine. When she works privately one-on-one she selects a collection of tunes to fit different people—their stride length, tempo, and mood, as well as their personal likes and dislikes. She uses music of many genres from Mozart to Sinatra to David Byrne. She uses the music often with visual cues, like stepping over a white line. She says the visual cueing is also a form of rhythmic structure.

The Mark Morris Dance Group also runs its own program for Parkinson's patients—Dance for Parkinson's disease. David Leventhal, a veteran Mark Morris dancer who teaches workshop classes, says the focus of the program is "to enrich and stimulate people to move." The approach is more aesthetic than therapeutic, although there are clear therapeutic benefits. This program also uses music familiar to the patients and pieces with structure. They don't pick compound meters but simple ones like 4/4 time. Leventhal believes that it's very important that the class uses live music and says, "Music has a way of accessing the imagination in a way that simple iteration of dance steps does not."[25] And dance, the Mark Morris workshop leaders recognize, taps into something primal. Indeed, evolutionary science links dance and music. To watch a class doing a square dance, smiling with pleasure, is testimony to the success of the program. Participants say they have more confidence in moving. The Mark Morris group is replicating the Parkinson's program with forty-five other classes around the world.

Dr. Concetta Tomaino attests to the effectiveness of

music therapy with language as well as movement for treating Parkinson's:

> The rhythmic timing of music can imbue a sense of speech timing that allows somebody to clearly articulate and take their time to make themselves understood. When people sing they tend to use a lot more breath support. And so the intuitiveness of singing allows for a lot more breath support and improved articulation that can really facilitate speech in somebody with Parkinson's.[26]

Michael Thaut believes special attention "must be given to rhythm as the most essential structural and organizational element of music."[27] Parkinson's damages both articulation and the breath support that patients need to speak intelligibly. What makes music such excellent medicine for this disorder? It could be the rhythm. It's known that the auditory system is a very fast sensory-processing system—faster, for example, than the visual system; it's very sensitive to temporal information processing. Thaut and his colleagues suggest that the sensitivity of our motor systems to sound may have developed during evolution so we could use the way we process what we hear to improve our ability to organize and control our movements and even speech. Perhaps Parkinson's patients who receive music therapy utilizing rhythm are inadvertently taking advantage of this ancient wiring in the human brain.

It's not just in motor performance and speech that the role of rhythm—rhythmic *patterns*—seems key, but also in cognitive functions such as attention and memory. This is another area

Michael Thaut is studying. Research by others has pointed to the role of rhythm in focusing attention. When we remember a song, we're not just recognizing it. We're remembering the patterns and temporal structure.[28] And research by Diana Deutsch at the University of Southern California has shown that some of the organizational processes used in memory formation for music also apply to nonmusical memory.[29] So music may well be able to activate memory processes.[30] Imagine the potential for Alzheimer's and dementia patients.

At the Center for Music and Neurologic Function, Connie Tomaino worked with an elderly woman who clearly had little memory left for most details of her life. But when Connie played a fragment of melody from an old Italian song on her accordion, the woman immediately played the song back on an electronic keyboard. She was accurate with the notes.[31]

Tomaino says part of music's power to trigger memory is due to association. This patient, for instance, had often sung the Italian song in her younger days. But the patterns of music are also involved. She says, "So this combination of what music allows somebody to hold on to, this information of structure, of recall, recognition are all part of memory that are still available to somebody with dementia. And I believe that music holds particular elements together for the individual to make those responses possible."[32]

Tomaino's elderly patient had the last word about music and memory in her session. She emphatically said, "Once you get it in your head it stays there."

Many patients have musical memory that lasts longer than other forms of memory. But what about other kinds of memory? Could music reactivate those as well?

There has been an explosion of research in a field called social neuroscience that has shown the medial prefrontal cortex (MPFC) is the brain region for self-referential activity—how we maintain our sense of self, feel emotion, think, and infer what others are thinking. It's also known that the medial prefrontal cortex is the last area of the brain to atrophy with Alzheimer's disease. Cognitive neuroscientist Petr Janata had already demonstrated that musical tonality is mapped in the prefrontal cortex. So Janata theorized that the MPFC is a kind of command center for emotions, for music, and for memory—even nonmusical memory. He used fMRI brain imaging to test subjects' responses to music that triggered strong autobiographical memories. He pinpointed each subject's response to a song. Janata found that "what seems to happen is that a piece of familiar music serves as a sound track for a mental movie that starts playing in our heads. It calls back memories of a particular person or place, and you might all of a sudden see that person's face in your mind's eye. Now we can see the association between those two things—the music and the memories."[33]

The tests showed the MPFC was indeed activated by the autobiographical music. Janata says at the very least this shows specially selected music can bring pleasure to Alzheimer's patients. "We're talking an iPod, a playlist, and the potential to make these people at least transiently happy. If you can have quality of life improvements for that little money, that's huge."[34]

In clinical settings right now, it's the immediate effects of music on memory that are noticeable. But Tomaino says if music therapy is used over time on dementia patients, there is potential to create more lasting change. Some years ago, the Institute for Music and Neurologic Function did a study funded by the New

York State Department of Health. The goal was to look at people with mid- to late-stage dementia and see if music could produce improvement in long-term memory function. Over ten months, the results showed that many mental status scores actually improved. Moreover, not only were people's long-term memories stimulated, but their short-term memories and attention also greatly improved. So we actually can imagine a future when music can be used to slow the degenerative neurologic effects of Alzheimer's disease and dementia. And the future seems to be getting closer.

There's also growing evidence—at least anecdotal—that music helps children with autism. One theory is that the structure and patterns of music complement the cognitive abilities and proclivities of people with autism, which include a strong desire to create patterns. Even autistic children who are hypersensitive to sound often respond well to music. It's difficult to create studies to assess the benefits of music therapy with autism because individual behavior varies so greatly. But therapists and parents testify to results. And music therapy has become a part of many programs for children with autism. In the late twentieth century, Dr. Alfred Tomatis, a French ear, nose, and throat doctor, gained international renown for developing a method of auditory training to target disorders including auditory-processing problems, learning disorders, and autism. Tomatis believed that impaired hearing function is the root cause of many ailments.

There are now other specially designed commercially available music/sound listening programs, based on the concept that the whole body can be affected through the ear using special stimuli. There is no hard proof of their comparative effectiveness, but anecdotal evidence suggests that more research might yield evidence that auditory stimuli can retrain the brain to process auditory information more effectively.

Alex Doman, the founder and CEO of the company Advanced Brain Technologies, explained the principles behind its program designed for children with autism. He said it's largely based on neuroscience, psychoacoustics, and the experience of the company's research team. The program uses music that is specially chosen, arranged, recorded, modified, and delivered with a specialized method. Over a period of time, the program is designed to train the auditory system by gradually increasing and then decreasing tempos. This provides variability in dynamics and tone density. The high-definition recording and headphone delivery is part of a process that gives listeners a sense of where they are and where each instrument is in space. And the program progressively exposes the listener to first all frequencies within the human hearing range, then low frequencies, then frequencies heard in spoken language, then high frequencies, and then back in reverse sequence. The company is also doing a pilot program using this technique with soldiers suffering from post-traumatic stress disorder.[35]

Advanced Brain Technologies recently supported a pilot study conducted by June Rogers with the British National Health Service in Liverpool, testing whether its music listening program delivered through a specialized bone conduction audio system could help toilet train autistic children. The results surprised even Alex Doman. Seven out of eleven children were fully potty trained within the time of the protocol. And the other four all made gains. Now the plan is to do a larger clinical trial with more rigorous research design.[36] Doman sees more and more scientific research supporting the use of music and sound to help autistic patients.[37]

We now know that the auditory system affects the autonomic nervous system. And research by psychiatrist Stephen Porges postulates that the operation of the autoimmune system is linked to social behavior. Porges, who's also a specialist in autism, posed the polyvagal theory. "Vagal" refers to the vagus, a nerve that's part of the autonomic nervous system. "Poly" means the nerve has two branches—one that evolved later in evolution and is unique to mammals. This new branch controls communication and social behavior, including listening. With autism, the fight-or-flight response of the sympathetic nervous system is overactive, so listening/communication skills and social behavior are affected.[38]

Porges has tested ways in which sound can help people with autism, who tend not to be able to look other people in the eye. He once exposed twenty autistic people to engineered speech and music, removing low-frequency sounds, which the body tends to interpret as signaling danger. He also exaggerated vocal intonations. After forty-five minutes, all but one of the subjects began making eye contact. The effect lasted at least a week just from the one exposure.[39]

The idea of tailoring specific music treatments for different medical and psychological problems is already emerging in commercial applications. Vera Brandes, a former music producer, is now director of Music Medicine Research at the

Paracelsus Private Medical University in Salzburg, Austria. She calls herself "the first musical pharmacologist." She became interested in the work of an expert in chronobiology. Chronobiology studies the effect of time on biological rhythms of body functions. In terms of music, the *time* we listen to a piece of music—whether we're in an up or down cycle of circadian rhythms—will make a difference in our response, Brandes surmised. She has formed a company to produce prescriptive music based on the hypothesis that we perceive music as pleasant if structures in the music sync up with our biological cycle. The point is that both the "regulatory process in the music and the physiological data of the listener" need to be analyzed to produce specific therapeutic effects, Brandes explains. Her company has developed proprietary techniques to do just that. So a doctor can send a diagnosis and information about the patient. The patient then gets prescriptive music loaded on a portable player along with a listening protocol with instructions about what time to listen. The music is also proprietary, chosen according to a system that analyzes certain structural aspects. It's specially composed. Brandes does not want to use music that could be known to the patient and have associations. That would dilute or confuse the effect. The company's music "pharmacy" has remedies designed for depression, pain management, anxiety, hypertension, and some types of cardiac arrhythmia. Brandes says pilot studies conducted at Paracelsus University show improvement as a result of the music program. For example, 89 percent of the subjects showed a reduction in depressive symptoms of an average of 60 percent.

Brandes was driven to investigate the healing powers of music through her own experience. She was in a bad car crash and broke two of her vertebrae. Doctors said she'd be immobilized for up to fourteen weeks. Brandes happened to be sharing her hospital room with a Buddhist whose friends came and chanted every day. After just two weeks, an MRI scan showed her spine was healed. That's when she decided to try and create prescriptive music that could be tailored to people according to their medical needs.[40]

This is a pioneering venture. And it's fair to say the jury is still out as far as results are concerned. Critics point out that even with instructions for when to listen, there's still no way to control what the patient is doing at any given time in addition to taking the musical medicine. Still, this may well be a harbinger of the future, with even more refined methods for prescriptive music to come.

The conviction of several very established music scientists is that the most effective music prescriptions will involve not just listening but making music—experiencing it directly by singing or playing an instrument. Barry Bittman believes in recreational music making—active engagement.[41] Neurologist Gottfried Schlaug points to the research proving *doing* music can change the brain. And Stefan Koelsch, a senior research fellow in neurocognition at the University of Sussex in Brighton, agrees that doing is the thing. Koelsch is working on participatory musical treatments for depression. And he sees even more potential for prescriptive music in the future. He says, "Physiologically, it's perfectly plausible that music would affect not only psychiatric conditions but also endocrine, autonomic and autoimmune disorders. I can't say music is a pill to abolish these diseases. But my vision is that we can come up with things to help. This work is so important. So many pills have horrible side effects, both physiological and psychological. Music has no side effects, or no harmful ones."[42]

Concetta Tomaino remembers the day, in the 1980s, when virtually nothing was known about music perception and the brain, when she and Oliver Sacks saw the effects of music on stroke and Parkinson's patients and they asked each other what was going on. Until the early 1990s, scientists who wanted to study music and the brain were rejected by research institutions. Nobody would pay them to run the experiments. What a change. Tomaino thinks that within five years people will be getting music therapy prescribed in rehabilitation clinics. Music therapy has been around since the 1950s, but it wasn't based on knowledge of the brain. That's no longer the case, but the public perception has yet to catch up, Tomaino says:

> I think the general public still sees music and music therapy as therapeutic music groups that somebody enjoys and participates in, that has a short-lived therapeutic purpose, but not the long-range purpose that music therapy now has today; it's goal oriented. Music therapy is now really treatment based in the sense that we assess the patient's needs and then use music and the components of music to really achieve nonmusical goals, such as improved motor function or improved psychological health and well-being. So the goals really aren't for the music per se, but to achieve other therapeutic aims.[43]

When one looks at the big picture of all the advances in the use of music for therapeutic purposes over the last decade, it's easy to use the term "revolutionary." Recent discoveries bear out what Herbert Spencer, the British philosopher and sociologist, once said: "Music must take rank as the highest of the fine arts—as the one which, more than any other, ministers to human welfare."

⊱ CHAPTER 12 ⊰

The Next Wave?

God dazzles us by an excess of truth.
Music carries us to God in default of truth.

—ST. THOMAS AQUINAS

⊶⊷

I'm lying on what looks like a massage table. But it's vibrating in synchronization with the music that I'm hearing through headphones. I'm experiencing a form of sound/music therapy that's supposed to be altering my brainwaves. This is new territory for me. I am certainly beyond the realm of what's considered established "hard science." But people who use this specially designed sound table, especially over a period of time, report lower anxiety, reduced tension and pain, and increased focus and a shift in consciousness to a meditative state.

I know respected musicians who believe wholeheartedly in the principles on which methods or programs using specially produced musical sound to achieve therapeutic effects are based, so I am trying it for myself. Programs like this are becoming increasingly popular and there's a great deal of curiosity surrounding them. Therapies like this are part of the journey of exploration into the impact of sound and music.

The study of music as a therapeutic tool has become territory that's really subdivided according to the type and degree of expertise and by the perspective of researchers and practitioners. It's important to distinguish between them: neuroscientists, whose research is providing the foundation for new types of music therapy, and music therapists, certified and licensed specifically in *using* music with patients to affect psychological, physical, and neurologic changes. Music practitioners are playing to soothe or relax a patient, but are not certified. And there are specialists in the use of sound and music for healing in ways not yet generally part of the scientific and medical mainstream. Perhaps these methods can be considered the new "alternative" music/sound therapy.

We know that sound can change the structure of matter. Remember that sand particles on a metal plate or water form different patterns depending on the sound or music played. And sound can make a wineglass vibrate with the frequency that fits the natural frequency of the glass. Our bodies, too, have natural frequencies in different parts. Our bones, for instance, vibrate to music.

The table I tried was created by a company called the Center for Neuroacoustic Research, headed by Dr. Jeffrey Thompson. Thompson, a chiropractor, is one of the sound-therapy practitioners now offering programs, methods, and products to the general public. Again, this is not an area in which there are published scientific papers. But to some degree, their work is based on generally recognized scientific and medical fact.

Dr. Thompson's vibrating sound table is part of his method. The goal is to create physical resonance in the body. Thompson, who also composes music, was practicing as a chiropractor when he wondered if he could use sound tones to get vertebrae to resonate. The idea was to shift through frequencies until he found the exact one that would cause the vertebrae creating pain to resonate. He could tell when he was successful by muscle testing. A stressed muscle is weak. When the pain is reduced, the muscle is stronger. So he tried it. And he says even he was somewhat surprised when he found it worked. He began to try it on more and more patients. He says he was having such good results that he decided to devote all his time to sound therapy. He sold his practice and moved from Virginia to California, where, he says, "People don't drag you away for these ideas."[1]

Researchers in this relatively new field of study called physioacoustics are using frequencies of sound to create sympathetic vibration in the deep tissues of the body. The same principle—creating physical resonance—is at work in Dr. Thompson's sound table. It's been found that low frequencies—too low to hear—cause the body to vibrate. The body becomes like a receiver in a stereo system. And it vibrates only in areas specifically responsive to those frequencies. For example, the muscles of the back will vibrate when stimulated by sounds with a frequency range between 45 and 55 hertz, but not the leg muscles.

This technique originated in Finland in the mid twentieth century. The Finnish war department was looking not at ultrasound (sound pressure that uses very high frequency sound) but at low frequencies that can be used, conceivably, to break down a wall or blow up a submarine. Despite the intentions of the original researchers in the field, psychoacoustics is used by Dr. Concetta Tomaino, director of the Institute for Music and Neurologic Function at Beth Abraham Medical Center in New York City, to help relieve pain in patients. She explained that "a lot of pain other than joint pain is related to muscle spasms or tightness. If the nerve is inflamed, the muscles around tighten to protect the nerve. And that causes pain." The institute has chairs that deliver the vibration. Tomaino says, "What happens is you feel like this vibration is going through your body in waves, but actually while the vibrations are presented to the whole body, only part of your body is vibrating at that specific frequency. You can feel the effects right away."

Tomaino, who feels that psychoacoustic techniques hold much potential for this application, had her team do a pilot study using physioacoustics on multiple sclerosis (MS) patients. The results were impressive: One patient who had chronic spasms went for several entire days with no spasms at all.

Another idea behind the work of Dr. Thompson and others working in the field of sound therapy is brain wave entrainment (BWE). As we've learned, the human brain entrains to rhythm. Humans—and it seems some other species—can synchronize to rhythm. When the auditory system receives impulses from the pulse of a rhythm or tonal vibration, the pattern of neuron signals—or firings—changes. EEG technology now allows us to record those firings and measure brain wave patterns. The brain is constantly producing electrical impulses that have frequencies. The categories of brain wave, defined according to the frequency, are beta, alpha, theta, and delta. And they're associated with certain states of consciousness. Beta is our normal waking, functioning state of consciousness. And the others progress through stages of relaxation, meditative states, dreaming sleep, or deep meditation and deep dreamless sleep. EEG studies show that it's possible to change brain wave speed by exposure to external sound pulses.

Here's the basic concept: First, the pulses are timed to the initial speed of the subject's brain waves. Once entrainment is achieved with a dominant pulse, then the speed of the external pulse is changed, and the speed of the brain waves shifts along with it. There are, in fact, research studies on how groups of cells in one area of the brain have firing frequencies in synchrony with groups of cells in another area. So for that idea to work in brain wave entrainment, rhythmic sound would trigger similar frequency cell firing in the auditory system. And the auditory system in turn would recruit other areas— emotion regulation, attention executive functions.[2] Neuroscientist Larry Parsons thinks it's doubtful that so much of the brain could work in parallel on so many time and frequency scales from a single stimulus. However, he proposes another possibility that "the rhythmic auditory function inspires the listener to breathe or move in rhythmic patterns, which then drives rhythmic cycling of groups of cells."[3] One recent study supports this hypothesis.[4]

Consciousness, of course, is a subject of much debate beyond the scope of this discussion. Generally neurologists tend to believe that consciousness—or awareness—is the result of electrochemical neurological activity. But even comatose patients can have some brain activity. There's no objective way to measure states of consciousness with an instrument. And there's no region or structure in the brain identified with consciousness. EEG patterns measure only electroneurological activity, from which one can infer states of consciousness based on historical associations. And neuroscience does not yet know how brain activity that we're aware of differs from the brain activity driving unconscious actions. It's important to note these mysteries surrounding the concept of consciousness in considering techniques intended to *change* states of consciousness.

One other discovery also informs Dr. Thompson's work and that of many others working in sound therapy. A phenomenon called binaural beats was discovered in the nineteenth century by a German researcher, Heinrich Wilhelm Dove. These are apparent tones that the brain "hears"—but not in the normal sense. They are produced when two tones at slightly different frequencies are heard separately. For example, if a tone at 315 hertz is played from one speaker and a tone at 325 hertz from another speaker, the brain "hears" a beat at 10 hertz. It's a phantom tone. Binaural beats were not the subject of much attention until the 1973 publication in *Scientific American* of a paper by Gerald Oster, a researcher at Mount Sinai Hospital in New York City. Oster examined all the research to date and presented new theories. He said that processing binaural beats involves different neural pathways than conventional hearing does. And he believes that they are a powerful tool for neurological and cognitive research.

Oster hooked subjects up to EEG machines while they heard binaural beats through headphones. Once the brain waves locked on the pulse, Oster changed the pulse and the brain waves changed—entrainment. Since then, it's been widely reported that binaural beats can enable brain wave entrainment and help induce changes in consciousness. They are used by many sound-therapy practitioners.

Dr. Jeffrey Thompson says what's going on with brain wave entrainment using binaural beats is that the two hemispheres of the brain are being synchronized. He goes on to say that "hemisphere synchronization is a big thing. That's where mystical experience and spiritual revelation happens. Now when you listen to sound tracks with binaural beat information on the tracks, your brain is in a state of prolonged synchronicity of the hemispheres for the first time in our species' biological evolution."[5]

That's a strong statement. But it's the kind of statement that's drawing more and more people to experiment with sound and music therapy. Opera singer Irene Gubrud, who also teaches meditation and breathing courses, says that for the purpose of attaining calm, relaxed, alert states, Thompson's technique of using physical resonance and brain entrainment "works more quickly than meditation. It's a superhighway. It takes you there faster."[6] As for my own half hour on the sound table listening to Thompson's specially designed and produced music, I definitely found that I relaxed very quickly. I was certainly conscious and aware of my surroundings, but I also felt rather on the verge of dreaming or sleeping.

Brain wave entrainment does not get good reviews from many scientific and medical experts. Dr. Barry Bittman, whose work and research focuses on relieving stress through musical sound, dismisses it as "pop science from the seventies and eighties." He points out that one can change one's brain waves to alpha simply by closing one's eyes. And he says there's no good data that correlates brain wave entrainment with a meaningful outcome.[7]

Still, there's no denying the recent surge of interest—perhaps due to the desire especially in America to find new ways to facilitate meditation and ultimately further spiritual growth. Meditation, according to some spiritual traditions, can lead people to experience a loss of the sense of self, a loss of ego, and oneness with the divine. It also can alleviate anger and anxiety. If sound and music can be used to achieve these goals more easily or quickly than through countless hours of meditative practice, then of course they are appealing.

This is surely not the first generation to be intrigued by this use of musical sound. Our ancestors and some traditional cultures today use sound and music not only for physical healing but to try to attain deeper states of consciousness. Dr. Thompson points out that shamanic drumming is usually about four and a half to five cycles per second. Five cycles per second is a low theta brain wave, considered typical of a dream state.[8] Ethnomusicologist Kay Kaufman Shelemay says she believes that one of the most powerful domains in which music operates is healing:

One finds that many healers are, just by virtue of the ways in which they heal, musicians. In many African cultures, there are studies in Zimbabwe, Malawi, Ghana, and a number of places in sub-Saharan Africa where music and healing are simply joined. Often there is intense music making that puts someone into an altered state. And during that period of altered consciousness a healer actually exorcises a spirit or a malady. One also has other traditions where music can guard against something bad happening or an illness. One finds this in some of the Indonesian rituals that involve the music of the gamelan, which sends people into trance and the trance then protects the people. In one Balinese ritual, music is used to appeal to the deities if there's some misfortune.[9]

Music, healing, and spirituality have had a connection since the beginning of human history. Chanting and toning are used across cultures to alter states of mind. And prayers are usually sung or chanted. Today's sound "healers" all seem to have spiritual as well as therapeutic purposes. I met Kimba Arem, who makes recordings with the renowned alternative medicine advocate Dr. Andrew Weil. Arem plays the didgeridoo, an aboriginal instrument that may be the oldest in the world. The aboriginals say it connects them to "the dream time." The "didge," as it's called, is a wind instrument that requires a special breathing technique to play. One inhales through the nose at the same time as breathing out into the mouthpiece. It can produce a great range of overtones. The sound is unique and unmistakable.

Arem trained as a musician as a child, but was studying to become a scientist and taking premed courses when she had a near-death experience after a car accident. Soon after, she discovered the didgeridoo and changed her life course to become a sound healer. Arem uses the didge in conjunction with crystal bowls, drums, and bells. She believes that sound therapy can cause real physical change. She says she's seen it work in dramatic ways with clients. Her intention is to use sound therapy to direct energy to parts of the body that need healing. At the least, it can relax and calm the client. Arem also hopes, like Dr. Thompson and others in the sound-therapy field, that the techniques can lead people to higher states of consciousness that awaken greater creativity and awareness of connectedness with other living creatures.[10]

Whatever spiritual experiences people may have through sound and music therapies, whatever their interpretations of those experiences, they often seem to be describing trance states—when we feel that we're outside of our individual, normal "selves" somehow. Neuroscientists do not know what lies behind so-called trance states, which sometimes are associated with the absence of normal pain response. Judith Becker, an ethnomusicologist at the University of Michigan, has done extensive research on the connection between music and trance across cultures. She defines this state as "a type of consciousness that lies outside 'our normal waking consciousness.'"[11]

Becker notes that there's been very little scientific study of trancing because it's considered strange and dangerous, and it's mistrusted by established religions. But Becker thinks recent theories of the biology and neurophysiology of consciousness have created a way to think of trance and its accompanying music as a kind of consciousness linked to strong emotion and a loss of our sense of "I-ness," as she puts it.

Neuroscientist Petr Janata is intrigued about music's relationship to trance states. Janata is conducting a study trying to understand what is going in the brain when people are "in the groove," so caught up in either listening to or performing music that they've lost that "sense of 'I-ness.'" Janata says, "I think the element of social engagement is a really important component of it. Playing music together is really powerful." But he thinks one can be in the groove by oneself, too, listening to music through headphones, for instance.

Janata acknowledges the scientific stigma regarding trance. But he says, "I think one can really pin it down to this rigorous definition where I think what it's telling us is that there's something about music that engages our sensory motor systems in conjunction with our emotional systems. So it's just this complete engagement of the brain's perception and action systems. I do think it has something to do with the rhythmic properties. And that's really what we're after. We're testing the idea that it's this seamless coupling of perception and action that allows the emotion system to activate."[12]

But it's challenging to study trance in a controlled, scientific setting. If a person seems engaged and taps his or her feet, moving to the music, is that really a sign of trance? As Daniel Levitin pointed out, foot tapping seems a long way from spiritual experience or trance state. And as yet, no one has looked at neurochemical changes that might occur during apparent trance states.

Still, Janata says it's possible to make correlations between EEG recordings of certain brain regions and neurochemical changes. His study is ongoing. But his theory seems similar to that of Judith Becker—trance states induced by music are linked to emotion.

Many musicians are interested in trance. David Byrne made the documentary *Ilê aiyé* or *The House of Life* about candomblé, the Afro-Brazilian trance religion. He told Daniel Levitin that he's fascinated by trance music partly because he thinks "there's a lot of popular secular music that borrows from sacred music because of the way it generates a kind of trance state or a transcendent state in the listener. So you see through the crack in the door or whatever. You can see that, wow, this music is taking me to a place that generates all those kind of vaguely spiritual feelings—like I've gone outside myself. And music is often talked about in spiritual terms. So I feel something is going on here."[13]

In this discussion for *Seed* magazine, Daniel Levitin pointed out that chanting and practicing breath control can have similar effects, creating a sense that we are not in our conscious mind and that thoughts are not under our conscious control. Levitin reminded Byrne that nobody really knows why music or rhythm is able to induce this state. He said, "We do know a little bit, neurologically, about what's happening. We know there's a suppression of frontal-lobe activity. We can measure changes in alpha waves and gamma waves and things like this. But those are really descriptions, not explanations."

Levitin also offered a theory:

It does seem to have something to do . . . with this balance between seeking order and predictability and violating that order and predictability. And when you have a complex pattern of rhythm or pitch, which is what music is, you relinquish some of your control. You're in a state of relaxation, you're following along this stream of sounds. You're making yourself vulnerable, giving in to the music. And you're lulled into this state of half sleep, half wakefulness. It's a powerful experience to have with other people.[14]

Grateful Dead percussionist Mickey Hart says his experience performing is what drove him to explore the transformative and healing powers of vibration and musical sound: "To get up on stage and play is addictive; it's very much like opium. It feeds those parts of the brain and psyche that create consciousness and awareness. When we hit a good rhythm, our consciousness is transformed; you're dancing with the vibratory world."[15]

Cellist Michael Fitzpatrick told me about a trance he experienced during a performance when he was quite young:

> It just seemed like the whole of the cosmos came into me, and it felt like a tornado kind of just went through my whole body. I heard the sound of my cello change, some other voice almost. And I just went into this trance that was unlike anything I'd experienced to that point in my life. So that was sort of my introduction into what I think in sports they would refer to as going into the zone. Once you're in that zone, time is experienced differently, bodily states are experienced differently, and you can actually go into these very deep states of ecstasy or bliss, whatever you want to call it. But they're very peaceful states.[16]

Richard Hawley said when he's performing he sometimes feels he's entered another state of mind: "You don't realize where you are sometimes."[17]

Bobby McFerrin recalled a passage in the Bible that speaks to the power of music to induce trancelike states: "I think it's in the first book of Samuel, about David and Saul, when Saul started to have these fits of temper and David would play to soothe him, which is biblical testimony to the power of music, how it can change a person's mood." He thinks his mother knew this instinctively: "When I was a little kid growing up she knew this whole thing about musical therapy and how it can change your moods. Whenever I was sick, she would give me two things. She'd give me medicine and music, 'cause she knew that the medicine would take care of the pains of my body and the music would distract me. You know, music feels really good to me. It's like my own personal medicine cabinet."[18]

And McFerrin has had personal experiences that felt like music was putting him into a kind of trance, times when the music and the rhythm shifted something inside:

> I've had musical moments, my own sort of private moments when I've locked myself into some motif. And it literally feels like I've gotten to a place where I'm no longer singing. It's like it's coming through. You've worked yourself up into this place and it keeps going, keeps going, and even though I might be thinking to myself, how long is this going to go, I'm almost afraid to even intrude on what's happening. You know, I don't want to let it go.

In one sense, we have moved from considering music as a healing force to talking about music as a spiritual medium. Modern Western science makes such a distinction, yet in another sense, healing and spirituality *are* connected. We find that connection in human history and in traditional cultures today. Neuroscientist Daniel Levitin writes in his book *The World in Six Songs* about the evolutionary changes that gave humans a "musical brain—an enlarged prefrontal cortex, and all the myriad bilateral connections with cortical and subcortical areas." He continues:

> With these evolutionary changes came self-consciousness ... which brought with it spiritual yearnings and the ability to consider that there might be things more important than one's own life. I believe that a particular kind of music— songs associated with religion, ritual, and belief—served a necessary function in creating early human social systems and societies. Music helped to infuse ritual practices with meaning, to make them memorable, and to share them ... this yearning for meaning lies at the foundation of what makes us human.[19]

Music is an integral part of our being. So it seems reasonable to believe that it can be healing and transforming in a variety of ways. In the last couple of decades, science has made amazing advances in defining some of those ways. No doubt in years to come, it will define others. It's right to be cautious in making claims for treatment or cure by using therapies that may not have been examined with scientific rigor. But there are also those who believe we've lost something by drawing too rigid a boundary between music and the wider role it can play in our lives.

⊰ CHAPTER 13 ⊱

Beyond the Concert Hall

Music is a higher revelation than all wisdom and philosophy. Music is the electrical soil in which the spirit lives, thinks, and invents.

—LUDWIG VON BEETHOVEN

ᛌᛐ

S cience has given us a new perspective on our connection to music. It's reminding us that music offers so much more than entertainment. I was lucky because from earliest childhood, I was surrounded by music, immersed in it. It was an integral part of my life, even though I had no aspirations to become a professional musician. I heard live music as a part of daily life. I listened as my father improvised on the piano, playing with music. And I had an inkling that music is some kind of magic sound, another kind of language.

Over the time I've spent learning about the new science of music, I've been struck by how scientists and musicians alike keep coming back to the thought that our ancestors somehow knew something about music that we have lost. They knew it wasn't just for professionals up on a stage performing for the rest of us to pay money to hear. Music is for everyone.

The social role of music is a common theme among musicians. Bobby McFerrin said, "The most wonderful thing about music is that it's not really meant to be kept close to the breast, as they say. You know it's not for yourself alone. I think music is something to be shared with people."[1]

Daniel Barenboim speaks of music as a social educator:

Music teaches us many things. Music teaches us first of all that you can't go it alone. Even a single melody played by one unaccompanied instrument is in dialogue with itself. And the minute you have two voices, as in something relatively simple like the Bach two-part inventions, you see that the two voices can be in accord, saying more or less the same thing, or they can be in contradiction with each other. One of them can even be subversive, as when one voice plays something beautifully long and legato and the other keeps on repeating a staccato statement. Nothing is completely independent. Dependency is very negative because as long as there's one on top, there is also one at the bottom. And independence in the negative sense of the word means not caring about anything. A voice that thinks it is completely independent says, "I'm here; I'm independent; I'm alone; I am the melody; I don't care about rhythm, to hell with them." Between the two there's a third way that I like to call interdependence. Music teaches us that everything is connected. Nothing is really disconnected.[2]

Mickey Hart comes back to the unifying power of vibration and rhythm. "You are a multidimensional vibratory being in a world of rhythm," he says. "Everything goes better with a good rhythm." After a concert, Hart tells the audience to "take this and do something good with it. Hug your kids. Be kind. Music is a wonder and it's magic; it borders on magic."[3]

Many of the neuroscientists I've met who specialize in music/brain research are musically trained themselves. They play music and they understand from a personal as well as professional point of view what goes on when people play music together. Petr Janata says that for him being in a jam session playing with other people is a special experience. For him, getting "in the groove" with other musicians has a deep emotional and social impact.[4]

Daniel Levitin, a saxophone player, often participates in jam sessions. Levitin believes that music has a deeply rooted social purpose. He points to tribal communities that use music to form community. He says, "It's almost ironic that today technology and culture have taken us to where we all have our little ear-buds and we listen to music in private, given that for tens of thousands of years the only way music was experienced by humanity was communally."[5]

The Old Testament was initially recounted orally through music. Harvard ethnomusicologist Kay Kaufman Shelemay finds it significant that societies through history and across cultures have used music to record their history. She says these songs are particularly famous in parts of West Africa. And there's a similar song tradition in Serbia and other parts of the former Yugoslavia. There, some of the songs last two hours, telling stories of battles, famous victories, and historical encounters.

Shelemay points out that music can bring us together both in communities into which we're born and to form new communities when we want to argue against something. Music, she says, is a vehicle to forge coalitions.[6]

We see music used every day to help bring people together. Military bands march. Church congregations sing. Kids on the playground sing spontaneously. But at the same time, formal music programs are victims of budget cuts. Cognitive archaeologist Steven Mithen thinks this is regrettable: "I think we neglect music at our peril. Music is such an important way for building both personal well-being and the well-being of groups. That if we don't engage people in music, especially from a young age, somehow they're losing something of the human experience and somehow we threaten the well-being of our societies. So it's made me really sort of an evangelist for more music in schools."

Another important fact about the music of our ancestors— and even music outside of the world of modern performance in Western societies—is that it was more ubiquitous and more spontaneous at the same time. Bobby McFerrin thinks we've lost a great deal of those qualities today and that we could learn from more traditional cultures:

I think that this is one of the reasons why I'm so attracted to the music of Africa, because music is such a part of life. My friend Yo-Yo Ma, when we first met, we had many, many conversations about this, and he knew that he had to do something for his music making that would take him into a deeper place in himself. And so he went to Africa, and he went to Botswana, just sort of out in a village somewhere. Lots and lots and lots of music making. When he arrived in this village, there was an interpreter trying to explain to the villagers that Yo-Yo Ma was going to play a concert at seven thirty at this place somewhere. And they had a hard time comprehending this for two reasons. One, they didn't understand why they had to wait to hear music. And why do we have to leave where we are to go somewhere else to hear it? Because music was so integrated into their life, they had no concept of performance. You know people were simply getting together and playing and they were celebrating everything. They were celebrating life, birth, harvest, hunting, everything.[7]

McFerrin said this story really changed his thinking about what it means to be a musician.

McFerrin, among some other great musicians, believes strongly in the importance of improvisation, spontaneously inventing music on the spot. He tells another story about Yo-Yo Ma in Africa. The cellist visited a shaman and was so struck by his music that he asked the shaman to sing a particular song again so that Yo-Yo Ma could write it down in musical notation. McFerrin relates:

The shaman's singing and Yo-Yo says, "Stop, wait, I need to write this down." So he writes it down, and he says, "Play it again. I want to make sure that I got it right." And the shaman sings and Yo-Yo is saying, "But that's not the piece you sang before." And the shaman laughed and he said, "Well, the first time I sang it, there was a herd of antelope in the distance. And a cloud was passing over the sun."[8]

In the few minutes that had elapsed since he sang, the clouds had moved, the wind had shifted, and the people were feeling different; the song would not be the same a second time. The song could not be separated from the people and the surrounding world. Beyond the concert hall, indeed. McFerrin sees the lesson for our world today:

So, this is the part that we've lost, is that every time a piece of music is played, you know one time there's a herd of antelope and one time there's not. And we turn in these cookie-cutter performances. Everything is so laid down and regimented and locked in and so rehearsed that they squeeze the life out of it. I think that's the part that we've lost. Improvisation is the key to it, I think. Improvisation is not head knowledge. It's heart knowledge. Basically, improvisation is simply motion. You sing one note and you keep singing note after note after note. And anyone can do that, whether they know or understand music or not. You don't have to know scales, modes, theory. Kids don't. They sing.[9]

Aaron Berkowitz, an ethnomusicologist and neuroscientist who's also an MD, is fascinated by the subject of improvisation and its relationship to language. He says that improvisation struck him as the clearest analogy to spontaneous language.

Berkowitz did fMRI scans of improvisers and found that Broca's area and other areas associated with spontaneous speech were also activated during improvisation. Berkowitz explains improvisation as having two aspects—free-form creativity combined with knowledge about musical elements and forms. He quotes the pianist Robert Levin, a renowned classical improviser, describing his improvisation of a cadenza (an ornamental passage played or sung by a soloist):

> As the orchestra starts to play the approach to the cadenza I start to think, "Well, how am I going to begin this?" . . . And in some wild way, I move back and forth over the material: this, that, something, but very often the orchestra arrives at the 6-4 chord and I think, "I don't have any idea what I'm going to do, except that I've got to start *now*."[10]

But Berkowitz reports that Levin can also analyze clearly what he does in terms of music theory when he performs a cadenza. So there seems to be internalized "head knowledge," to use Bobby McFerrin's term. But the "heart knowledge" takes over in the heat of the moment.

Physicist Stephon Alexander makes a fascinating analogy between quantum mechanics and improvisation. Quantum theory, he says, is based on probability. In quantum mechanics, there's the idea that everything exists in a wave of probability. And, Alexander reminds us, music is all about waves and time. As a jazz musician, he realized that improvisation in music is all about probability. Neither the performers nor the listeners know exactly where the music is going. Yet there's still a kind of direction. Alexander believes that in this sense musical improvisation may be echoing nature:

> If you now take that to the domain of quantum mechanics, you can say, well, maybe nature is improvising, and maybe we think the best we could ever do is make probabilistic statements, but nature's smarter than us. And maybe, you know, this wave-like property of the probability of matter existing in quantum mechanics, that interpretation, it might be cooler to think of it as an improvisation. So that's one way in which I like to link in improvisation, especially if the universe was really cool and funky. Then the universe would be a really good jazz improviser.[11]

British rock musician Richard Hawley says that improvising with other musicians shifts him into a special state:

> There's a great feeling in a way. It's like being in a group where you all listen to each other. It's like a great football [soccer] team. It's like Zen in a way. With football, we get eleven players that seem to be thinking as one. It's like that with a group of people making music that are kind of improvising. There is a magical feeling. Are the synapses not just in your own head? You can see kind of an idea or hear it and people follow, you know.[12]

As we've seen, Parsons and other neuroscientists are very interested now in the study of how music works on multiple brains. They want to understand the details of what's going on when we experience and play music together, what happens when we're grooving in a jam session or at a rock concert. Parsons realized that most of the earlier work on brain imaging with musicians had been with solo activity. So even before he scanned Jarvis Cocker as he sang along with Richard Hawley's guitar, Parsons had studied two singers in two scanners. He compared the scans to what happened when one singer sang by himself or with a piano. He found that "singing with a human produced much more intricate, complicated patterns of behavior than singing with the piano. Because there was ongoing negotiation. And compared to singing alone, the singing with another person activated a series on the left side of the brain—executive functioning areas, sequencing areas, auditory areas, and motor areas."[13]

Music can synchronize our brain states. Parsons thinks his results reflect the role that music has played through human history in shaping social communication and cooperation: "If you think about primitive cultures, people collecting around the campfire or the central meeting place, singing, dancing, mimicking animal species, narrating stories," he says, "all together, everybody participating all at the same time in this complicated broadband mix of social communication, that's where music probably really is in its natural setting."

Bobby McFerrin tries to re-create that experience in a concert hall. He says:

You're working in a hall, three thousand seats, whatever the capacity is. Most of them don't know each other, you know? Maybe they come in, you know, couples and families, whatever, but they don't know one another. But within a ninety-minute span, you can create a community of people who will walk out singing with perfect strangers . . . the music that took place might have come out of me, but it went into them and became all of us and we took that out. And that's the wonderful thing.[14]

It must be wonderful to be able to transmit music to others in that way. But as a listener I've had the kind of experience McFerrin describes. There have been moments in a concert hall when I heard great music performed by great artists that live in my memory as transformative. I truly felt the boundaries between the musicians and my fellow audience members and me dissolve. I was transformed. Perhaps my brain state was synchronized by the music with that of all the others in the auditorium. But these are spiritual experiences. And I agree with Bobby McFerrin when he says that music *is* fundamentally spiritual.

Yet I find it wonderful that modern science is giving us confirmation and more reasons than ever before to incorporate music into every aspect of our lives. In the future, we will likely turn to music not just for entertainment or emotional solace, but for healing—both physical and mental. And, because of science, we will have a deeper understanding than ever before of how music truly can transform us—both as individuals and together. Its potential seems boundless. I also believe that the mystery and magic of music will always remain. It is awesome. And we will always be awestruck when music is at its best and when we deeply listen.

ACKNOWLEDGMENTS

I want to thank all the scientists and musicians who gave so generously of their time and expertise to help me understand the interaction of music with the brain, body, and nature. I owe to them my own full appreciation of the importance of music and the groundbreaking research now under way. For their extraordinary support in teaching me how to convey the material I am especially grateful for the help of neuroscientist Lawrence M. Parsons and music theorist Richard Porterfield. I'm also indebted to neuroscientists Jamshed Bharucha, Daniel J. Levitin, and Aniruddh Patel, who also graciously agreed to write the Foreword for this book. For their talent, inspiration, and willingness to share their profound knowledge of music, I am grateful to Bobby McFerrin, Maestro Daniel Barenboim, Jarvis Cocker and Richard Hawley, Dame Evelyn Glennie, and Daniel Bernard Roumain (DBR). For their friendship, support, and advice over the years of developing the television program *The Music Instinct: Science & Song* and then this book, I am deeply grateful to Miriam Kartch, Carl Schachter, David and Eugenia Ames, Alecia Evans, Mary Milton, and Leopold Godowsky III. I also greatly appreciate the encouragement and support of Irene Gubrud, Mary Rodgers Guettel, Joel Lester, Mary Luehrsen, the late Michael Small, Eugene Becker, and Bill and Judith Moyers. I'm very fortunate to have received invaluable support and advice from Nancy Peske and Carmen Harra. For helping me learn to play the cello and further my understanding of the language of music, I thank my teacher Clara Kim. I am indebted to my television colleagues without whom I could not

have made *The Music Instinct* and hence this book. They include Marga-
ret Smilow, Junko Tsunashima, Kristin Lovejoy, Sunoko Aoyagi Bow-
ers, Jesssica Bari, Steven Stoke, and Donna Marino.

I would also like to thank my editor/publisher at Walker Books,
George Gibson, for great support, intelligence, and advice. I also thank
Jacqueline Johnson at Walker for her skillful editing and contributions.

My profound gratitude goes to the great music that I have been
privileged to hear all my life.

NOTES

Introduction: Music Matters

1. Tom Fritz, of the Max Planck Institute for Human Cognitive and Brain Sciences in Leipzig, Germany, conducted this study in Cameroon in 2006. Fritz collaborated with his colleague, Stefan Koelsch. The results were published in the March 19, 2009 issue of *Current Biology*. Fritz et al., "Universal Recognition of Three Basic Emotions in Music," 573–6.
2. Barry Bittman, director, Mind-Body Wellness Center, phone conversation with Elena Mannes, November 17, 2009.

Chapter 1: Feel the Sound

1. Interview with Daniel Levitin for *The Music Instinct: Science and Song*, PBS (aired June 2009).
2. Interview with Michael Fitzpatrick for *The Music Instinct*.
3. Interview with Bobby McFerrin for *The Music Instinct*.
4. Ibid.
5. Evelyn Glennie Web site, www.evelyn.co.uk.
6. Interview with Evelyn Glennie for *The Music Instinct*.
7. Irene Gubrud interview with Elena Mannes, November 3, 2009, and June 2010.
8. Interview with Daniel Bernard Roumain (DBR) for *The Music Instinct*.
9. Interview with Maestro Daniel Barenboim for *The Music Instinct*.
10. Interview with Sheila Woodward for *The Music Instinct*; Woodward and Guidozzi, "Intrauterine Rhythm and Blues?" 787–90.
11. Interview with Sheila Woodward for *The Music Instinct*.

12. Interview with Bobby McFerrin and Brian Greene for *The Music Instinct.*
13. Irene Gubrud interview with Elena Mannes.
14. Interview with Michael Fitzpatrick for *The Music Instinct.*
15. Interview with Brian Greene for *The Music Instinct.*
16. Interview with Bobby McFerrin for *The Music Instinct.*
17. Interview with Michael Fitzpatrick for *The Music Instinct.*

Chapter 2: Music Plays the Body

1. Sequence and interview with Daniel Levitin for *The Music Instinct.*
2. Interview with Robert Zatorre for *The Music Instinct*; Blood and Zatorre, "Intensely Pleasurable Responses," 11818–23.
3. These findings were presented at the Music and the Brain symposium produced by the Cleveland Clinic Arts and Medicine Institute in collaboration with Lincoln Center Presents, October 30, 2009, in New York.
4. S. Strogatz and I. Stewart, "Coupled Oscillators and Biological Synchronization," *Scientific American*, December 1993, 102–17.
5. M. Mockel et al., "Immediate Physiological Responses of Healthy Volunteers to Different Types of Music: Cardiovascular, Hormonal and Mental Changes," *European Journal of Applied Physiology and Occupational Physiology* 69, no. 3, 274.
6. B. Miluk-Kolasa, Z. Obminiski, R. Stupnicki, and L. Golec, "Effects of Music Treatment on Salivary Cortisol in Patients Exposed to Pre-Surgical Stress," *Experimental and Clinical Endocrinology* 102, no. 2 (1994): 118–20.
7. Norman M. Weinberger, "The Musical Hormone," *Musica Research Notes* 4, issue 2 (Fall 1997) Regents of the University of California, http://www.musica.uci.edu/mrn/V4I2F97.html.
8. Barry Bittman interview with Elena Mannes, November 17 and November 25, 2009; Bittman et al., "Composite Effects of Group Drumming Therapy," 38–47.
9. Barry Bittman interview with Elena Mannes.
10. Barry Bittman interview with Elena Mannes, November 17 and

November 25, 2009; Bittman et al., "Recreational Music-Making Modulates the Human Stress Response," BR31–40.

Chapter 3: The Brain Plays Music

1. Interview with Daniel Levitin for *The Music Instinct*; Levitin, *This Is Your Brain on Music*, 74–75.
2. Interview with Daniel Levitin for *The Music Instinct*.
3. Interview with Jamshed Bharucha for *The Music Instinct*.
4. Emmanuel Bigand, "The Influence of Implicit Harmony, Rhythm and Musical Training on the Abstraction of 'Tension-Relaxation Schemas' in Tonal Musical Phrases," *Contemporary Music Review* 9, 123–37.
5. J. A. Grahn and J. B. Rowe, "Feeling the Beat: Premotor and Striatal Interactions in Musicians and Non-Musicians During Beat Perception," *Journal of Neuroscience* 29, no. 23 (2009): 7540–8.
6. Interview with Daniel Levitin for *The Music Instinct*; Levitin, *This Is Your Brain on Music*, 150–54.
7. Interview with Daniel Levitin for *The Music Instinct*.
8. Robert Zatorre, "Neural Specializations for Tonal Processing," The Biological Foundations of Music, *Annals of the New York Academy of Sciences* 930 (2001): 193–210.
9. Gerald Langner, "Neuronal Mechanisms Underlying the Perception of Pitch and Harmony," *Annals of the New York Academy of Sciences* 1060 (2005): 50–52.
10. Interviews with Lawrence Parsons for *The Music Instinct*; Parsons et al., "Brain Basis of Piano Performance," 199–215.
11. Parsons et al., "Brain Basis of Piano Performance"; interviews with Lawrence M. Parsons for *The Music Instinct*.
12. Interview with Lawrence Parsons for *The Music Instinct*; L. M. Parsons, "Exploring the Functional Neuroanatomy of Music Performance, Perception, and Comprehension," *Annals of the New York Academy of Sciences* 930 (2001): 211–31.
13. Interview with Robert Zatorre for *The Music Instinct*.
14. Interview with Lawrence Parsons for *The Music Instinct*.

15. Petr Janata interviews with Elena Mannes, 2009, 2010. P. Janata et al., "Cortical Topography of Tonal Structures Underlying Western Music," *Science* 298 (December 13, 2002).

16. Interview with Daniel Levitin for *The Music Instinct*.

17. Ibid.; Levitin, *This Is Your Brain on Music*, 123, 189–91. Vinod Menon and Daniel J. Levitin, "The Rewards of Music Listening: Response and Physiological Connectivity of the Mesolimbic System," *NeuroImage* 28, no. 1 (May 26, 2005): 175–84.

18. Salimpoor et al., "Rewarding Aspects of Music Listening," e7487.

19. Interview with Daniel Levitin for *The Music Instinct*.

20. Interview with Robert Zatorre for *The Music Instinct*.

21. Interview with Lawrence Parsons for *The Music Instinct*.

22. Interview with Richard Hawley for *The Music Instinct*.

23. Interview with Lawrence Parsons for *The Music Instinct*.

Chapter 4: Is Music Our Genetic Birthright?

1. Interview with Bobby McFerrin for *The Music Instinct*.

2. Interview with Daniel Levitin for *The Music Instinct*.

3. Interview with Bobby McFerrin for *The Music Instinct*.

4. Interview with Daniel Levitin for *The Music Instinct*; Levitin, *This Is Your Brain on Music*, 41.

5. Interview with Jamshed Bharucha for *The Music Instinct*.

6. Interview with Sandra Trehub for *The Music Instinct*; S. E. Trehub, "Musical Predispositions in Infancy: An Update," in R. Zatorre and I. Peretz, eds., *The Cognitive Neuroscience of Music* (Oxford: Oxford University Press, 2003), 3–20.

7. McDermott et al., "Individual Differences Reveal the Basis of Consonance," 1035–41.

8. Sandra Trehub interview with Elena Mannes, spring 2010.

9. Ibid.

10. L. Trainor, C. Tsang, and V. Cheung, "Preference for Sensory Consonance in 2- and 4-Month-Old Infants," *Music Perception* 20, no. 2 (Winter 2002): 187–94.

11. Laurel Trainor interview with Elena Mannes, summer 2010.

12. Sandra Trehub interview with Elena Mannes, spring 2010.

13. N. Masataka, "Preference for Consonance over Dissonance by Hearing Newborns of Deaf Parents and of Hearing Parents," *Developmental Science* 9, issue 1 (January 2006): 46–50, article first published online: 16 Dec 2005 doi:10:1111/j.1467-7687. 2005.00462x.

14. Interview with Sandra Trehub for *The Music Instinct*.

15. Interview with Kathleen Wermke for *The Music Instinct*.

16. R. A. Polverini-Rey, "Intrauterine Musical Learning: The Soothing Effect on Newborns of a Lullaby Learned Prenatally," unpublished doctoral dissertation, California School of Professional Psychology, Los Angeles, 1992.

17. E. Hannon and Laurel J. Trainor, "Music Acquisition: Effects of Enculturation and Formal Training on Development," submitted for publication August 2010.

18. Laurel Trainor interview with Elena Mannes, summer 2010.

19. I. Winkler, G. P. Haden, O. Ladnig, I. Sziller, and H. Noning, "Newborn Infants Detect the Beat in Music," *Proceedings of the National Academy of Sciences*, January 6, 2009, doi:10.1073/pnas.0809035106.

20. D. Deutsch, T. Henthorn, E. Marvin, and H-S. Xu, "Absolute Pitch among American and Chinese Conservatory Students: Prevalence Differences and Evidence for a Speech-Related Critical Period," *Journal of the Acoustical Society of America* 119 (2006): 719–22; D. Deutsch, "Absolute Pitch—a Connection Between Music and Speech?" *Bulletin of Psychology and the Arts* 4 (2003): 19–21; Deutsch, "The Puzzle of Absolute Pitch," 200–204.

21. J. R. Saffran, "Absolute Pitch in Infancy and Adulthood: The Role of Tonal Structure," *Developmental Science* 6, no. 1 (2003): 37–49.

22. Interview with Sandra Trehub for *The Music Instinct*.

23. Interview with Kay Shelemay for *The Music Instinct*.

24. Ibid.

25. Interview with Bobby McFerrin for *The Music Instinct*.

26. Interview with Daniel Bernard Roumain (DBR) for *The Music Instinct*.

27. Interview with Tom Fritz for *The Music Instinct*; Tom Fritz, of the

Max Planck Institute for Human Cognitive and Brain Sciences in Leipzig, Germany, conducted this study in Cameroon in 2006. Fritz collaborated with his colleagues, Stefan Koelsch et al. The results were published in the March 29, 2009 issue of *Current Biology*. Fritz et al., "Universal Recognition," 573–6.

28. Ibid.

Chapter 5: Agony and Ecstasy: How We Listen

1. Interview with John Sloboda for *The Music Instinct*.
2. Sloboda, *The Musical Mind*, 50–51.
3. John A. Sloboda, "Music Structure and Emotional Response: Some Empirical Findings," *Psychology of Music* 19 (October 1991): 110–20, doi:10.1177/0305735691192002.
4. Sridharan et al., "Neural Dynamics of Event Segmentation in Music," 521–32.
5. "Mapping the Brain's Response to Music: fMRI Studies of Musical Expectations," *Stanford Scientific*, February 17, 2008: Sridharan et al., "Neural Dynamics of Event Segmentation in Music," 521–32.
6. Interview with Richard Hawley for *The Music Instinct*.
7. S. Koelsch, T. Fritz, and G. Schlaug, "Amygdala Activity Can Be Modulated by Unexpected Chord Functions During Music Listening," *NeuroReport* 19, no. 18 (December 2008): 1815–19.
8. Interview with Daniel Levitin for *The Music Instinct*.
9. Sridharan et al., "Neural Dynamics of Event Segmentation in Music," 521–32.
10. Salimpoor et al., "Rewarding Aspects of Music Listening," e7487.
11. C. Krumhansl, "An Exploratory Study of Musical Emotions and Psychophysiology," *Canadian Journal of Experimental Psychology*, 51(1997): 336–52. Examples of selections were "Spring" from *The Four Seasons* by Vivaldi (happy), *Adagio for Strings* by Samuel Barber (sad), and *Night on Bald Mountain* by Mussorgsky (fear).
12. Parsons et al., "Brain Basis of Piano Performance," 199–215.
13. Interview with Jarvis Cocker and Richard Hawley for *The Music Instinct*.

14. Ibid.

15. Interview with Alinka Greasley for *The Music Instinct.*

16. Interview with John Sloboda for *The Music Instinct.*

17. P. Janata, J. Birk, J. Van Horn, M. Leman, B. Tillmann, and J. Bharucha, "Cortical Topography of Tonal Structures Underlying Western Music," *Science* 298 (December 13, 2002): 2267–70. Janata has created a computer model of what he calls "the torus," representing all the Major and minor keys of Western music. And he's built a computer program showing how pieces of music move through this tonal space.

18. Interview with Lawrence Parsons for *The Music Instinct.*

19. Lawrence Parsons interviews with Elena Mannes, 2008, 2009, 2010.

Chapter 6: Mind-Bending Notes: Can Music Make Us Smarter?

1. Interview with Gottfried Schlaug for *The Music Instinct.*

2. Interview with Robert Zatorre for *The Music Instinct.*

3. P. Schneider, M. Scherg, H. Günter Dosch, H. J. Specht, A. Gutschalk, and André A. Rupp, "Morphology of Heschl's Gyrus Reflects Enhanced Activation in the Auditory Cortex of Musicians," *Nature Neuroscience* 5, no. 7 (July 2002): 688–4, published online June 17, 2002, doi:10.1038/nn871.

4. Interview with Gottfried Schlaug for *The Music Instinct;* G. Schlaug, A. Norton, K. Overy, and E. Winner, "Effects of Music Training on Brain and Cognitive Development," *Annals of the New York Academy of Science* 1060 (2005): 219–30.

5. Interview with Gottfried Schlaug for *The Music Instinct.*

6. Interview with Robert Zatorre for *The Music Instinct.*

7. Interviews with Steven Mithen and Lawrence Parsons for *The Music Instinct.*

8. Interview with Robert Zatorre for *The Music Instinct.*

9. Rauscher et al., "Music and Spatial Task Performance," 611. A pilot study finds that preschool children given music training display significant improvement in spatial reasoning ability. An experiment with college students finds that after listening to a Mozart

sonata, they experience a significant although temporary gain in spatial reasoning. F. Rauscher, G. Shaw, L. Levine, and K. Ky, paper presented at the American Psychological Association, 102nd Annual Convention, Los Angeles, Calif., August 12–16, 1994. A follow-up study (Stage II) finds that after eight months of keyboard lessons, preschoolers demonstrated a 46 percent boost in their spatial reasoning IQ. This gain does not occur in those without music training. F. H. Rauscher, G. L. Shaw, and K. N. Ky, "Listening to Mozart Enhances Spatial-Temporal Reasoning: Towards a Neurophysiological Basis," *Neuroscience Letters* 185, (1995): 44–47. A follow-up to the first Mozart study confirms that listening to Mozart improves spatial reasoning, and that this effect can increase with repeated testing over days. However, the effect may not occur when music lacks sufficient complexity.

10. K. L. Hyde, J. Lerch, A. Norton, M. Forgeard, E. Winner, A. C. Evans, and G. Schlaug, "The Effects of Musical Training on Structural Brain Development," *Annals of the New York Academy of Science* 1169 (2009): 182–6. K. L. Hyde, J. Lerch, A. Norton, M. Forgeard, E. Winner, A. C. Evans, and G. Schlaug, "Musical Training Shapes Structural Brain Development," *Journal of Neuroscience* 29 (2009): 3019–25.

11. Interview with Gottfried Schlaug for *The Music Instinct*.

12. Ibid. Catherine Y. Wan and Gottfried Schlaug, "Music Making as a Tool for Promoting Brain Plasticity Across the Life Span," *Neuroscientist* 16, no. 5 (2010): 566–77.

13. There is some debate about the effectiveness of these fetal listening devices. See R. Saslow, "Experts Split over Usefulness of Prenatal Audio Devices," *Washington Post*, October 12, 2009, JSO Online .com/features/health/64003902.html.

14. C. E. H. Dirix, J. G. Nijhuis, H. Jongsma, "Aspects of Fetal Learning and Memory," *Journal of Child Development* (July–August 2009), article first published online July 15, 2009, doi:10.1111/j.1467-8624.2009.01329.x.

15. A. Krueger, "Music Is Instrumental in Teaching," *San Diego Union-Tribune*, December 19, 2009, http://signonsandiego.

16. B. H. Helmrich, "Window of Opportunity? Adolescence, Music, and Algebra," *Journal of Adolescent Research* 25, no. 4 (July 2010): 557–77, published online before print April 29, 2010, doi:10.1177/0743558410366594.

17. Interview with Sebastian Jentschke for *The Music Instinct*.

18. Jentschke et al., "Investigating the Relationship of Music and Language in Children," 231–42. Interview with Sebastian Jentschke for *The Music Instinct*.

19. Jentschke et al., "Children with Specific Language Impairment," 1940–51.

20. Interview with Sebastian Jentschke for *The Music Instinct*.

21. Interview with Robert Zatorre for *The Music Instinct*.

22. Interview with Daniel Bernard Roumain (DBR) for *The Music Instinct*.

23. Ibid.

24. Ibid.

25. Interview with Maestro Daniel Barenboim for *The Music Instinct*.

26. Interview with Stephanie Uibel for *The Music Instinct*.

Chapter 7: Music Speaks

1. Interview with Daniel Levitin for *The Music Instinct*. Levitin, *This Is Your Brain on Music,* 157–8.

2. Interview with Lawrence Parsons for *The Music Instinct*; Brown et al., "Music and Language Side by Side in the Brain," 2791–803.

3. Brown et al., "The Neural Basis of Human Dance," 1157–67.

4. Interview with Lawrence Parsons for *The Music Instinct*.

5. Interviews with Jarvis Cocker, Richard Hawley, and Lawrence Parsons for *The Music Instinct*.

6. Interview with Aniruddh Patel for *The Music Instinct*. A. D. Patel, J. R. Iversen and J. C. Rosenberg, "Comparing the Rhythm and

Melody of Speech and Music: The Case of British English and French," *Journal of Acoustical Society of America* 119, (2006): 3034–304; Patel, *Music, Language, and the Brain.*

7. Jentschke et al., "Investigating the Relationship of Music and Language in Children," 231–42.

8. Interview with Aniruddh Patel for *The Music Instinct*; Patel, *Music, Language, and the Brain.*

9. Mampe et al., "Newborns' Cry Melody," 1–4.

10. Interview with Sandra Trehub for *The Music Instinct.*

11. Schwartz et al., "Statistical Structure of Human Speech Sounds," 7160–8.

12. David Schwartz interview with Elena Mannes, August 2006.

13. Steven Pinker, *How the Mind Works* (New York: W. W. Norton, 1997).

14. Interview with Steven Pinker for *The Music Instinct.*

15. Ibid.

16. Ibid.

17. Interview with Robert Zatorre for *The Music Instinct.*

18. Interview with Aniruddh Patel for *The Music Instinct.*

19. Interview with Steven Mithen for *The Music Instinct.*

Chapter 8: Why Music?

1. Interview with Steven Mithen for *The Music Instinct.*

2. Mithen, *The Singing Neanderthals.*

3. Interview with Nicholas Conard for *The Music Instinct.*

4. Conard et al., "New Flutes," 737–40.

5. Interview with Nicholas Conard for *The Music Instinct*; Nicholas Conard interview with Elena Mannes, July 2010.

6. Wulf Hein interview with Elena Mannes, August 2010.

7. Charles Darwin, *The Descent of Man, and Selection in Relation to Sex*, 2 vols. (London: John Murray, 1871), 880.

8. Ibid.

9. Miller, "Evolution of Human Music," in Wallin et al., *Origins of Music*, 239–60.

10. Interview with Steven Mithen for *The Music Instinct.*

11. Mithen, *The Singing Neanderthals.*
12. Interview with Steven Mithen for *The Music Instinct.*
13. Ibid.
14. Ibid.
15. Ibid.
16. Ibid.
17. Laurel Trainor interview with Elena Mannes, August 2010. David W. Gerry, Ashley L. Faux, and Laurel J. Trainor, "Effects of Kindermusik Training on Infants' Rhythmic Enculturation," *Developmental Science* 13, no. 3 (2010): 545–51.
18. Interview with Sandra Trehub for *The Music Instinct.*
19. Interview with Lawrence Parsons for *The Music Instinct.*
20. Brown et al., "The Neural Basis of Human Dance," 1157–67. Brown et al., "Music and Language Side by Side in the Brain," 2791–803.
21. Interview with Steven Pinker for *The Music Instinct.*
22. Interview with Steven Mithen for *The Music Instinct.*
23. J. Blacking, *How Musical Is Man?* (Seattle: University of Washington Press, 1973).
24. Interview with Steven Mithen for *The Music Instinct.*
25. Interview with Daniel Levitin for *The Music Instinct*; Levitin, *This Is Your Brain on Music,* 265–67.
26. Interview with Daniel Levitin for *The Music Instinct.*

Chapter 9: Whale Songs, Elephant Bands, and Dancing Birds
1. Interview with Aniruddh Patel for *The Music Instinct.*
2. Ibid.
3. Ibid.
4. Ibid.
5. Ibid.
6. Ibid.
7. Isabelle Peretz, "Monkeys Have Tin Ears," *Science* 317 (August 3, 2007): 577.
8. Interview with Robert Zatorre for *The Music Instinct.*
9. Interview with Ofer Tchernichovski for *The Music Instinct.*

10. Ibid.

11. Ibid.

12. Ibid.

13. Interview with David Rothenberg for *The Music Instinct*.

14. Ibid.

15. Erich Jarvis interviews with Elena Mannes, Summer 2010. Kubikova et al., "Dopamine Receptors in a Songbird Brain," 741–69.

16. P. R. Hof, E. Van der Gucht, "Structure of the Cerebral Cortex of the Humpback Whale, *Megaptera novaeangliae* (Cetacea, Mysticeti, Balaenopteridae)," *The Anatomical Record* 290, no.1 (January, 2007): 1–31, doi:10.1002/ar.20407. PMID 1744119.

17. Patrick Hof interview with Elena Mannes, summer 2010.

18. Payne and McVay, "Songs of Humpback Whales," 585–97.

19. Scott McVay interview with Elena Mannes, summer 2010.

20. Ibid.

21. Payne and McVay, "Songs of Humpback Whales," 585–97.

22. Scott McVay interview with Elena Mannes, summer 2010.

23. Timothy E. Holy, Zhongsheng Guo, "Ultrasonic Songs of Male Mice," *PLoS Biology* 1 (November 2005), doi:10.1371/journal.pbio.0030386.

24. Erich Jarvis interview with Elena Mannes.

25. Ibid.

26. C. Traehol, R. Bonthoeun, C. Virak, M. Samuth, and S. Vutthi, "Song Activity of the Pileated Gibbon, *Hylobates pileatus*, in Cambodia," *Primate Conservation* 21 (2006): 139–44.

27. Interview with Lawrence Parsons for *The Music Instinct*.

28. N. I. Mann, K. A. Dingess, and P. J. B. Slater, "Antiphonal Four-Part Synchronized Chorusing in a Neotropical Wren," *Biology Letters* 2, no. 1 (March 22, 2006): 1–4.

29. Ibid.

30. Interview with Lawrence Parsons for *The Music Instinct*.

31. Anthony A. Wright and Jacquelyne J. Rivera, "Music Perception and Octave Generalization in Rhesus Monkeys," *Journal of Experimental Psychology: General* 129, no. 3 (September 2000): 291.

32. T. Sugimoto, H. Kobayashi, N. Nobuyoshi, Y. Kiriyama, H.

Takeshita, T. Nakamura, K. Hashiya, "Preference for Consonant Music over Dissonant Music by an Infant Chimpanzee," *Primates* 51, no. 1 (January 2010): 7–12, doi: 10:1007/s 20329-009-0160-3.

33. A. Chase, "Music Discriminations by Carp (*Cyprinus carpio*)," *Animal Learning & Behavior* 29, no. 4 (2001): 336–53.
34. S. Watanabe and K. Sato, "Discriminative Stimulus Properties of Music in Java Sparrows," *Behavioral Processes* 47, issue 1 (August 19, 1999): 53–57.
35. Snowdon and Teie, "Affective Responses in Tamarins."
36. Erich D. Jarvis, "Neural Systems for Vocal Learning in Birds and Humans: A Synopsis," *Journal of Ornithology* 143 (2007): S35–44.
37. E. Balaban, S. Edelman, S. Grillner, U. Grodzinski, E. D. Jarvis, J. H. Kaas, G. Laurent, and G. Pipa, "Evolution of Dynamic Coordination," in *Dynamic Coordination in the Brain: From Neurons to Mind*, C. von der Malsburg, W. A. Phillips, and W. Singer, eds, Strungmann Forum Reports, J. Lupp, series ed. (Cambridge, Mass.: MIT Press, 2010), 59–82.
38. Erich Jarvis interview with Elena Mannes, summer 2010.
39. Ibid.
40. Interview with David Rothenberg for *The Music Instinct*.
41. Scott McVay interview with Elena Mannes, summer 2010.

Chapter 10: The Music of the Spheres

1. J. Kepler, *Harmonices Mundi* (1619), translated by Charles Glenn Wallis, 1939.
2. Mark Whittle interview with Elena Mannes, summer 2009.
3. Mark Whittle, *Big Bang Acoustics*, University of Virginia: http://www.astro.virginia.edu/~dmw8f.
4. Ibid.; Whittle, *Cosmology*.
5. Dennis Overbye, "Scientists Develop the Universe's Baby Pictures," *New York Times*, May 24, 2002. N. W. Halverson, E. M. Leitch, C. Pryke, J. Kovak, J. E. Carlstrom, W. L. Holzapfel, M. Dragovan, J. K. Cartwright, B. S. Mason, S. Padin, T. J. Pearson, A. C. S. Readhead, and M. C. Shepherd, "Degree Angular Scale

Interferometer First Results: A Measurement of the Cosmic Microwave Background Angular Power Spectrum," *Astrophysical Journal* 568, no. 1 (March 2002): 38–45.

6. Overbye, "Scientists Develop the Universe's Baby Pictures."

7. "Phase" means the particular point in the cycle of a waveform, measured as an angle in degrees.

8. Hu and White, "The Cosmic Symphony," 44–53.

9. Whittle, *Big Bang Acoustics*.

10. Ibid.

11. Interview with Brian Greene for *The Music Instinct*.

12. John Dryden, "A Song for St. Cecilia's Day," 1687. Reprinted in *The Oxford Book of English Verse 1250–1900*, edited by Arthur Quiller-Couch. Oxford: Clarendon, 1919.

13. Whittle, *Big Bang Acoustics*; flute harmonics: http://www.phys.unsw .edu.au/music/flute/baroque/Fsharp4.baroque.html.

14. Whittle, *Big Bang Acoustics*.

15. Interview with Daniel Bernard Roumain (DBR) for *The Music Instinct*.

16. Interview with Maestro Daniel Barenboim for *The Music Instinct*.

17. Margulis, "Moved by Nothing," 245–76.

18. BigThink.com, June 19, 2008.

19. Interview with Brian Greene for *The Music Instinct*.

20. Stephon Alexander interview with Elena Mannes, summer 2009.

21. "What Do the Planets Sound Like?" *Science Line*, Physical Science Blog, by Ferris Jabr, posted February 22, 2010 (presentation by Greg Laughlin and Philip Glass at the Rubin Museum of Art, New York, February 21, 2010).

22. A. Burrows, E. Livne, L. Dessart, C. D. Ott, and J. Murphy, "A New Mechanism for Core-Collapse Supernova Explosions," *Astrophysical Journal* 640 (2006): 878.

23. A. Fabian et al. "A Deep Chandra Observation of the Perseus Cluster: Shocks and Ripples," 2003, *Monthly Notices of the Royal Astronomical Society*, in press; astro-ph/0306036v2.

24. Dennis Overbye, "Songs of the Galaxies and What They Mean," *New York Times,* August 3, 2004.

25. Interview with Brian Greene for *The Music Instinct.*

26. http://www-pw.physics.uiowa.edu/space-audio/sun-rings.

27. Mickey Hart interview with Elena Mannes, October 15, 2010.

28. http://www.mickeyhart.net/home/; "Mickey Hart's Music of the Universe Reveals the Sound of Supernova," http://berkeley labreport.blogspot.com/2010/01/mickey-harts-music-of-uni verse-reveals.html; http://www.sciencedaily.com/releases/2010/ 01/100129164526.htm.

29. Mickey Hart, *Rhythms of the Universe*; Mickey Hart interview with Elena Mannes, October 15, 2010.

30. Mickey Hart interview with Elena Mannes, October 15, 2010.

31. Mark Whittle interview with Elena Mannes, summer 2010.

32. Ibid.

33. BigThink.com, June 19, 2008.

34. http://www.goodreads.com/author/quotes/1429989.Richard_P_ Feynman.

35. http://personalpages.manchester.ac.uk/staff/jay.kennedy/#Links_ to_Papers_and_Files; "Scholars React to 'Plato Code' claims," *Philosopher's Magazine,* August 20, 2010, issue 51, http://www.phi losophypress.co.uk/?p=1454.

Chapter 11: Pain, Pills—or Music

1. Cooper Davis, "Classic Carly Simon, It's Never Been Gone," *Vine- yard Gazette,* October 23, 2009.

2. Claudius Conrad, "Overture for Growth Hormone: Requiem for Interleukin-6?" *Critical Care Medicine* 35, issue 12 (December 2007): 2709–13.

3. Dr. Claudius Conrad interview with Elena Mannes, summer 2010.

4. MSNBC.com, December 7, 2009, http://www.msnbc.msn.com/ id/309990170/.

5. Joanne Loewy, Cathrine Hallan, Eliezer Friedman, Christine

Martinez, "Sleep/Sedation in Children Undergoing EEG Testing: A Comparison of Chloral Hydrate and Music Therapy," *Journal of Peri-Anesthesia Nursing* 20, no. 5 (October 2005): 323–331.

6. "Music and the Brain: A Symposium," October 30, 2009, Cleveland Clinic Arts & Medicine Institute in collaboration with Lincoln Center Presents.

7. Ibid.

8. Mitchell Gaynor interview with Elena Mannes, summer 2010.

9. Ibid.

10. Bittman et al., "Recreational Music-Making: An Integrative Group Intervention."

11. Barry Bittman interview with Elena Mannes, November 17 and November 25, 2009. Bittman et al., "Composite Effects of Group Drumming."

12. Barry Bittman interview with Elena Mannes, summer 2010.

13. Bittman et al., "Recreational Music-Making Modulates the Human Stress Response," BR31–40.

14. Barry Bittman interview with Elena Mannes, summer 2010.

15. Ibid.

16. Interview with Concetta Tomaino for *The Music Instinct*.

17. Cooper Davis, "Classic Carly Simon."

18. Interview with Gottfried Schlaug for *The Music Instinct*. L. Zipse, S. Marchina, and G. Schlaug, "Melodic Intonation Therapy: Shared Insights on How It Is Done and Why It Might Help," *Annals of the New York Academy of Sciences* 1169 (2009): 431–36.

19. Ibid.

20. Interview with Robert Zatorre for *The Music Instinct*.

21. Thaut et al., "The Connection Between Rhythmicity and Brain Function."

22. Ibid.

23. Michael H. Thaut and Mitsumi Abiru, "Rhythmic Auditory Stimulation in Rehabilitation of Movement Disorders: A Review of Current Research," *Music Perception* 27, no. 4 (April 2010): 263–9;

Michael H. Thaut, "Neural Basis of Rhythmic Timing Networks in the Human Brain," *Annals of the New York Academy of Sciences* 999 (November 2003): 364–73; Michael H. Thaut, "The Future of Music in Therapy and Medicine," *Annals of the New York Academy of Sciences* 1060 (December 2005): 303–8.

24. Pamela Quinn interview with Elena Mannes, summer 2010.

25. David Leventhal interview with Elena Mannes, summer 2010.

26. Interview with Concetta Tomaino for *The Music Instinct*.

27. Thaut et al., "Auditory Rhythmicity Enhances Movement and Speech Motor Control," 162–72.

28. P. R. Cook, *Music, Cognition, and Computerized Sound: An Introduction to Psychoacoustics* (Cambridge, Mass: MIT Press, 1999).

29. D. Deutsch, "Organizational Processes in Music," in *Music, Mind and Brain*, ed. M. Clynes (New York: Plenum Press, 1982), 119–31.

30. Thaut, "Neurologic Music Therapy," 281–86.

31. Interview/sequence with Concetta Tomaino for *The Music Instinct*.

32. Interview with Concetta Tomaino for *The Music Instinct*.

33. Petr Janata, Jeffrey L. Birk, John D. Van Horn, Marc Leman, Barbara Tillmann, Jamshed J. Bharucha, "The Cortical Topography of Tonal Structures Underlying Western Music," *Science* 298 (December 13, 2002); Janata, "The Neural Architecture of Music-Evoked Autobiographical Memories," 2579–94; Petr Janata interview with Elena Mannes, summer 2010.

34. Nancy Brands Ward, "Your Brain on Music," *Sacramento News & Review*, May 14, 2009.

35. Alex Doman interview with Elena Mannes, summer 2010.

36. "Classical Music on iPods Helps Toilet Train Liverpool Children," *Liverpool Echo*, July 8, 2010.

37. Alex Doman interview with Elena Mannes, summer 2010.

38. S. W. Porges, "The Polyvagal Theory: Phylogenetic Contributions to Social Behavior," *Physiology & Behavior* 79 (2003): 503–13; Porges, "Neuroception: A Subconscious System for Detecting Threats and Safety," *Zero to Three* 32 (2004): 19–24; Ravi Dykema, "How Your

Nervous System Sabotages Your Ability to Relate: An Interview with Stephen Porges about His Polyvagal Theory," *Nexus*, March/April 2006.

39. Temma Ehrenfeld, "How Do You Feel Now? Emotional States: Technology Gives Autistic Kids a Hand," *Newsweek International*, February 28, 2005.

40. Vera Brandes interview with Elena Mannes, spring 2010.

41. Barry Bittman interview with Elena Mannes, summer 2010.

42. Stefan Koelsch quoted in "Composing Concertos in the Key of Rx," by Matthew Gurewitsch, *New York Times*, March 29, 2009.

43. Concetta Tomaino interview with Elena Mannes, summer 2010.

Chapter 12: The Next Wave?

1. Jeffrey Thompson interview with Elena Mannes, summer 2010.

2. Lawrence Parsons interview with Elena Mannes, summer 2010.

3. Ibid.

4. Alfredo Fontanini, PierFranco Spano, and James M. Bower, "Ketamine-Xylazine-Induced Slow (1.5Hz) Oscillations in the Rat Piriform (Olfactory) Cortex Are Functionally Correlated with Respiration," *Journal of Neuroscience* 23, no. 21 (August 27, 2003): 7993–8001.

5. Jeffrey Thompson interview with Elena Mannes, summer 2010.

6. Irene Gubrud interview with Elena Mannes, summer 2010.

7. Barry Bittman interview with Elena Mannes, summer 2010.

8. Ibid.

9. Interview with Kay Kaufman Shelemay for *The Music Instinct*; Judith Becker, "Music, Trancing and the Absence of Pain," in *Pain and Its Transformations*, ed. Sarah Coakley and Kay Kaufman Shelemay (Cambridge, Mass.: Harvard University Press, 2007).

10. Kimba Arem interview with Elena Mannes, December 10, 2009.

11. Becker, "Music, Trancing and the Absence of Pain," in *Pain and Its Transformations*.

12. Interview with Petr Janata for *The Music Instinct*.

13. David Byrne and Daniel Levitin, "The Singer/Songwriter and

the Neuroscientist Meet Up to Discuss Music," *Seed*, April 30, 2007.

14. Ibid.
15. Mickey Hart interview with Elena Mannes, October 14, 2010.
16. Interview with Michael Fitzpatrick for *The Music Instinct*.
17. Interview with Richard Hawley for *The Music Instinct*.
18. Interview with Bobby McFerrin for *The Music Instinct*.
19. Levitin, *The World in Six Songs*, 191–2.

Chapter 13: Beyond the Concert Hall

1. Interview with Bobby McFerrin for *The Music Instinct*.
2. Interview with Maestro Daniel Barenboim for *The Music Instinct*.
3. Mickey Hart interview with Elena Mannes, October 14, 2010.
4. Interview with Petr Janata for *The Music Instinct*.
5. Daniel J. Levitin, quoted in *Seed*, April 30, 2007.
6. Interview with Kay Kaufman Shelemay for *The Music Instinct*.
7. Interview with Bobby McFerrin for *The Music Instinct*.
8. Ibid.
9. Ibid.
10. Aaron Berkowitz, *The Improvising Mind: Cognition and Creativity in the Musical Moment* (Oxford, U.K.: Oxford University Press, 2010), viii.
11. Stephon Alexander quoted on BigThink.com, June 19, 2008.
12. Interview with Richard Hawley for *The Music Instinct*.
13. Interview with Lawrence Parsons for *The Music Instinct*.
14. Interview with Bobby McFerrin for *The Music Instinct*.

BIBLIOGRAPHY

Following are some of the books, articles, and scientific papers that have been helpful to me in learning about the science of music. The list is not comprehensive, but will be of use to readers interested in delving more deeply into the subject matter. Some of the readings are written for professionals in the field; some are more appropriate for an interested but not expert reader.

Avanzini, Giuliano, Luisa Lopez, Stefan Koelsch, and Maria Majno, eds. "The Neurosciences and Music II: From Perception to Performance," Annals of the New York Academy of Sciences 1060 (2005).

Ball, T., B. Rahm, S. B. Eickhoff, A. Schulze-Bonhage, O. Speck, and I. Mutschler, "Response Properties of Human Amygdala Subregions: Evidence Based on Functional MRI Combined with Probabilistic Anatomical Maps," PLoS ONE, no. 2, e 307. doi: 10:1371/journal .pone0000307. March 21, 2007.

Berkowitz, Aaron. The Improvising Mind: Cognition and Creativity in the Musical Moment. Oxford, England: The Oxford University Press, 2010.

Bharucha, J. J. "Neural Nets, Temporal Composites and Tonality" in The Psychology of Music, 2nd ed., ed. D. Deutsch. (New York: Academic Press, 1998).

Bharucha, J. J., M. Curtis, and K. Paroo. "Varieties of Musical Experience." Cognition 100 (2006): 131–73.

Bittman, B., MD, L. S. Berk, D. L. Felten, MD, J. Westengard, C. Simonton, MD, J. Pappas, MD, and M. Ninehouser. "Composite Effects of

Group Drumming Music Therapy on Modulation of Neuroendocrine-Immune Parameters in Normal Subjects." *Alternative Therapies* 7, no. 1 (January 2001): 38–47.

Bittman, B., MD, K. T. Bruhn, C. Stevens, J. Westengard, and P. O. Umbach. "Recreational Music-Making: A Cost-Effective Group Interdisciplinary Strategy for Reducing Burnout and Improving Mood States in Long-Term Care Workers." *Advances in Mind Body Medicine* 19, no. 3/4 (Fall/Winter 2003): 4–15.

Bittman, B., MD, C. Snyder, K. T. Bruhn, F. Liebfreid, C. K. Stevens, J. Westengard, and P. O. Umbach. "Recreational Music-Making: An Integrative Group Intervention for Reducing Burnout and Improving Mood States in First Year Associate Degree Nursing Students: Insights and Economic Impact." *International Journal of Nursing Education Scholarship* 1, article 12 (July 9, 2004).

Bittman, B., MD, L. Berk, M. Shannon, M. Sharaf, J. Westengard, K. J. Guegler, and D. W. Ruff. "Recreational Music-Making Modulates the Human Stress Response: A Preliminary Individualized Gene Expression Strategy." *Medical Science Monitor* 11, no. 2 (2005): BR31–40.

Bittman B., MD, L. Dickson, and K. Coddington. "Creative Musical Expression as a Catalyst for Quality-of-Life Improvement in Inner-City Adolescents Placed in a Court-Referred Residential Treatment Program." *Advances* 24, no. 1 (Spring 2009).

Blood, A. J., R. J. Zatorre, P. Bermudez, and A. C. Evans. "Emotional Responses to Pleasant and Unpleasant Music Correlate with Activity in Paralimbic Brain Regions." *Nature Neuroscience* 2 (1999): 382–7.

Blood, A. J., and R. J. Zatorre. "Intensely Pleasurable Responses to Music Correlate with Activity in Brain Regions Implicated with Reward and Emotion." *Proceedings of the National Academy of Sciences* 98 (2001): 11818–23.

Brown, S., M. J. Martinez, and L. M. Parsons. "The Neural Basis of Human Dance," *Cerebral Cortex* 16 (2006): 1157–67.

Brown, S., M. J. Martinez, and L. M. Parsons. "Music and Language Side by Side in the Brain: A PET Study of Generating Melodies and

Sentences." *European Journal of Neuroscience* 23 (2006): 2791–803. Images from study were issue cover illustration.

Coakley, Sarah, and Kay Kaufman Shelemay, eds. *Pain and Its Transformations: The Interface of Biology and Culture.* Cambridge, Mass.: Harvard University Press, 2007.

Conard, Nicholas J., M. Malina, and Suzanne C. Munzel. "New Flutes Document the Earliest Musical Tradition in Southwestern Germany." *Nature* 460 (August 6, 2009): 737–40, doi:10.1038/nature08169.

Deregnaucourt, S., P. P. Mitra, T. Lints, and O. Tchernichovski. "Song Development: In Search for the Error-Signal." *Annals of the New York Academy of Science* 1016. Special Issue: Neurobiology of Birdsong. Ziegler and Marler, eds. (2004): 348–63.

Deutsch, Diana. "The Puzzle of Absolute Pitch." *Current Directions in Psychological Science* 11, no. 6 (December 2002): 200–4.

———. "The Tritone Paradox: A Link Between Music and Speech." *Current Directions in Psychological Science* 6, no. 6 (December 1997).

———. "Speaking in Tones: Music and Language Are Partners in the Brain. Our Sense of Song Helps Us Learn to Talk, Read and Even Make Friends." *Scientific American Mind* (July/August 2010): 37.

Fritz, Tom, S. Jentschke, N. Gosselin, D. Sammler, I. Peretz, R. Turner, Angela D. Friederici, and S. Koelsch. "Universal Recognition of Three Basic Emotions in Music." *Current Biology* 19, no. 7 (March 19, 2009): 573–76.

Gaynor, Mitchell L., MD. *Sounds of Healing.* New York: Broadway Books, 1999.

Greene, Brian. *The Elegant Universe.* New York: Vintage Books, 2000.

Haas, R., and V. Brandes, eds. *Music That Works: Contributions of Biology, Neurophysiology, Psychology, Sociology, Medicine and Musicology.* New York: SpringerWienNewYork, 2009.

Hu, Wayne, and Martin White. "The Cosmic Symphony." *Scientific American* (February 2004): 44–53.

Janata, Petr. "The Neural Architecture of Music-Evoked Autobiographical Memories." *Cerebral Cortex* 19 (November 2009): 2579–94.

Jarvis, Erich D. "Bird Song Systems: Evolution." In *Encyclopedia of Neuroscience*, Vol. 2. edited by L. R. Squire, 217–25. Oxford, U.K.: Academic Press, 2009.

Jenny, Hans. *Cymatics*. Newmarket, N.H.: MACROmedia, 2001.

Jentschke, S., and S. Koelsch. "Musical Training Modulates the Development of Syntax Processing in Children." *NeuroImage* 47, no. 2 (August 15, 2009): 735–44. doi:10.1016/j.neuroimage.2009.04.090.

Jentschke, S., S. Koelsch, S. Sallat, A. D. Friederici, "Children with Specific Language Impairment Also Show Impairment of Music-Syntactic Processing." *Journal of Cognitive Neuroscience* 20, no. 11 (November 2008): 1940–51, doi:10.1162/jocn.2008.20135.

Jentschke, S., S. Koelsch, and A. D. Friederici. "Investigating the Relationship of Music and Language in Children: Influences of Musical Training and Language Impairment." *Annals of the New York Academy of Sciences* 1060 (December 2005): 231–42.

Khalfa, Stephanie, Simone Dalla Bella, Mathieu Roy, Isabelle Peretz, and Sonia J. Lupien. "Effects of Relaxing Music on Salivary Cortisol Level after Psychological Stress." *Annals of the New York Academy of Sciences: The Neurosciences and Music* 999 (November 2003): 374–376.

Koelsch, S., and Sebastian Jentschke. "Differences in Electric Brain Responses to Melodies and Chords." *Journal of Cognitive Neuroscience* 22, no. 10 (October 2010): 2251–62.

Koelsch, S., D. Sammler, S. Jentschke et al. "EEG Correlates of Moderate Intermittent Explosive Disorder." *Clinical Neurophysiology: Official Journal of the International Federation of Clinical Neurophysiology* 119, no. 1 (2008): 151–62.

Koelsch, S., and S. Jentschke. "Short-Term Effects of Processing Musical Syntax: An ERP Study." *Brain Research* 1212 (May 30, 2008): 55–62, http://www.ncbi.nlm.nih.gov/pubmed/18.

Koelsch, Stefan, et al. "A Cardiac Signature of Emotionality." *European Journal of Neuroscience* 26, no. 11 (2007): 3328–38. http://www.ncbi.nlm.nih.gov/pubmed/18.

Koelsch, Stefan, et al. "Untangling Syntactic and Sensory Processing:

An ERP Study of Music Perception." *Psychophysiology* 44, no. 3 (2007): 476–90. http://www.ncbi.nlm.nih.gov/pubmed/17.

Kraus, N., and B. Chandrasekaran. "Music Training for the Development of Auditory Skills." *Nature Reviews Neuroscience* 11 (August 2010): 599. doi:10.1038/nrn2882.

Kubikova, L., K. Wada, and E. D. Jarvis. "Dopamine Receptors in a Songbird Brain." *Journal of Comparative Neurology* 518 (2010): 741–69.

Lauterwasser, Alexander. *Water Sound Images*. Newmarket, N.H.: MACROmedia Publishing, 2006.

Levitin, Daniel J. *This Is Your Brain on Music: The Science of a Human Obsession*. New York: Plume/Penguin, 2007, Dutton 2006.

Levitin, Daniel J. *The World in Six Songs: How the Musical Brain Created Human Nature*. New York: Dutton, 2008.

Levitin, Daniel J., and Vinod Menon. "The Neural Locus of Temporal Structure and Expectancies in Music: Evidence from Functional Neuroimaging at 3 Tesla." *Music Perception* 22, no. 3 (spring 2005): 563–575.

Mampe, Birgit, Angela D. Friederici, Anne Christophe, and Kathleen Wermke. "Newborns' Cry Melody Is Shaped by Their Native Language." *Current Biology* 19 (December 15, 2009): 1–4.

Margulis, Elizabeth Hellmuth. "Moved by Nothing: Listening to Musical Silence." *Journal of Music Theory* 51, no. 2 (2007): 245–76.

McDermott, Josh H., Andriana J. Lehr, and Andrew J. Oxenham. "Individual Differences Reveal the Basis of Consonance." *Current Biology* 20 (June 8, 2010): 1035–41.

Miller, G. F. "Evolution of Human Music through Sexual Selection." In *The Origins of Music*, edited by N. L. Wallin, B. Merker, and S. Brown, 329–60. Cambridge: MIT Press, 2000.

Miluk-Kolasa, B., Z. Obminiski, R. Stupnicki, and L. Golec. "Effects of Music Treatment on Salivary Cortisol in Patients Exposed to Pre-Surgical Stress." *Experimental and Clinical Endocrinology* 102, no. 2 (1999): 118–20.

Mithen, Steven. *The Singing Neanderthals: The Origins of Music, Language, Mind and Body*. London: Weidenfeld & Nicolson, 2005.

Norton, A., L. Zipse, S. Marchina, and G. Schlaug. "Melodic Intonation Therapy: Shared Insights on How It Is Done and Why It Might Help." *Annals of the New York Academy of Science* 1169 (July 2009): 431–36.

Parsons, Lawrence M. "Music of the Spheres." *BBC Music Magazine,* November 2003: 34–39.

Parsons, L. M., J. Sergent, D. A. Hodges, and P. T. Fox. "Brain Basis of Piano Performance." *Neuropsychologia* 43 (2005): 199–215.

Patel, Aniruddh D. *Music, Language, and the Brain.* New York: Oxford University Press, 2008.

Patel, A. D. "Music, Biological Evolution, and the Brain." In *Emerging Disciplines,* edited by M. Bailar. Houston: Rice University Press, 2010: 91–144.

Patel, A. D., J. R. Iversen, M. R. Bregman, and I. Schulz. "Experimental Evidence for Synchronization to a Musical Beat in a Nonhuman Animal." *Current Biology* 19 (2009): 827–30.

Patel, A. D., J. R. Iversen, M. R. Bregman, and I. Schulz. "Studying Synchronization to a Musical Beat in Nonhuman Animals." *Annals of the New York Academy of Sciences* 1169 (2009): 459–69.

Patel, A. D., Iversen, J. R., Bregman, M. R., and I. Schulz. "Avian and Human Movement to Music: Two Further Parallels." *Communicative and Integrative Biology* 2, no. 6 (2009): 1–4.

Payne, R. S., and S. McVay. "Songs of Humpback Whales." *Science* 173, no. 3997 (August 13, 1971): 585–97.

Peretz, Isabelle, and Robert Zatorre, eds. *The Cognitive Neuroscience of Music.* Oxford, U.K.: Oxford University Press, 2003.

Peretz, I., J. Ayotte, R. J. Zatorre, J. Mehler, P. Ahad, V. B. Penhune, and B. Jutras. "Congenital Amusia: A Disorder of Fine-Grained Pitch Discrimination." *Neuron* 33 (2002): 185–91.

Pierce, John R. *The Science of Musical Sound.* New York: Scientific American Books, 1983.

Rauscher, F. H., G. L. Shaw, and C. N. Ky. "Music and Spatial Task Performance." *Nature* 365 (October 14, 1993): 611, doi:10.1038/365611a0.

Rothenberg, David. *Thousand Mile Song: Whale Music in a Sea of Sound.* New York: Basic Books, 2008.

———— *Why Birds Sing: A Journey into the Mystery of Birdsong*. New York: Basic Books, 2005.

Sacks, Oliver. *Musicophilia: Tales of Music and the Brain*. New York: Knopf, 2007.

Salimpoor, Valorie N., Mithcel Benovoy, Gregory Longo, Jeremy R. Cooperstock, and Robert J. Zatorre, "The Rewarding Aspects of Music Listening Are Related to Degree of Emotional Arousal." *PLoS One*, 4, no. 10: e7487, doi:101371/journal.

Schlaug, G., E. Altenmueller, and M. Thaut. "Music Listening and Music Making in the Treatment of Neurological Disorders and Impairments." *Music Perception* 27, no. 4 (2010): 249–50.

Schwartz, David A., Catherine Howe, and Dale Purves. "The Statistical Structure of Human Speech Sounds Predicts Musical Universals," *Journal of Neuroscience* 23, no. 18 (August 6, 2003): 7160–68.

Sloboda, John. *The Musical Mind: The Cognitive Psychology of Music*. Oxford, UK: Oxford University Press, 1985.

Sloboda, J. A., and P. Juslin, eds. *Music and Emotion: Theory and Research*. Oxford, UK: Oxford University Press, 2001.

Snowdon, Charles T., and David Teie. "Affective Responses in Tamarins Elicited by Species-Specific Music." *Biology Letters*, published online September 2, 2009. doi: 10.1098/rsbl.2009.0593.

Sridharan, D., D. J. Levitin, C. H. Chafe, J. Berger, and V. Menon. "Neural Dynamics of Event Segmentation in Music: Converging Evidence for Dissociable Ventral and Dorsal Networks." *Neuron* 55, no. 3 (August 2, 2007): 521–32.

Steinbeis, N., S. Koelsch, and J. A. Sloboda. "The Role of Harmonic Expectancy Violations in Musical Emotions: Evidence from Subjective, Physiological, and Neural Responses." *Journal of Cognitive Neuroscience* 18 (2006): 1381–93.

Storr, Anthony. *Music and the Mind*. New York: Ballantine Books, 1992.

"The Biology of Music," *Economist*, February 12–18, 2000.

Tchernichovski, O., T. Lints, S. Deregnaucourt, and P. P. Mitra. "Analysis of the Entire Song Development: Methods and Rationale." *Annals of the New York Academy of Science.* Special Issue: Neurobiology of Birdsong, ed. Ziegler and Marler. 1016 (2004): 348–63.

Thaut, Michael H. "Neurologic Music Therapy in Cognitive Rehabilitation." *Music Perception* 27, no. 4 (April 2010): 281–85.

Thaut, M. H., G. P. Kenyon, M. L. Schauer, and G. C. McIntosh. "The Connection Between Rhythmicity and Brain Function." *IEEE Engineering in Medicine and Biology* 18, no. 2 (March/April 1999): 101–8.

Thaut, M. H., and G. C. McIntosh. "Music Therapy in Mobility Training with the Elderly: A Review of Current Research." *Music Therapy* 1, no. 1 (Winter 1999).

Thaut, M. H., G. C. McIntosh, and V. Hoemberg. "Auditory Rhythmicity Enhances Movement and Speech Motor Control in Patients with Parkinson's Disease." *Functional Neurology* 16, no. 2 (2001): 162–72.

Thaut, M. H., G. C. McIntosh, and R. R. Rice. "Rhythmic Facilitation of Gait Training in Hemiparetic Stroke Rehabilitation." *Journal of the Neurological Sciences* 151 (1997): 207–12.

"The Music Enigma: Where Does It Come from and Why Do We Love It So Much?" *New Scientist*, February 23, 2008.

The Music Instinct: Science and Song (air date June 2009). http://www.pbs.org/wnet/musicinstinct/.

Trainor, Laurel J., and K. A. Corrigall. "Music Acquisition and Effects of Musical Experience." In *Music Perception*, edited by M. Reiss Jones, R. R. Fay, and A. M. Popper. New York: Springer, 2010.

Trainor, L. J., and R. Zatorre. "The Neurological Basis of Musical Expectations: From Probabilities to Emotional Meaning." In *Oxford Handbook of Music Psychology*, edited by S. Halten, I. Cross, and M. Thaut, 171–182. Oxford, UK: Oxford University Press, 2009.

Wallin, Nils L., Björn Merker, and Steven Brown, eds. *The Origins of Music.* Cambridge, Mass., and London: A Bradford Book, The MIT Press, 2000.

Wermke, Kathleen. "Relation of Melody Complexity in Infants' Cries to Language Outcome in the Second Year of Life: A Longitudinal Study." *Clinical Linguistics & Phonetics* 21, no. 11–12 (November–December 2007): 961–73.

Whittle, Mark. *Cosmology: The History and Nature of Our Universe.* Chantilly, Va.: The Teaching Company, 2008.

Woodward, S. C. "Critical Matters in Early Childhood Music Education." In *Praxial Music Education: Reflections and Dialogues,* edited by D. J. Elliott, 249–66. New York: Oxford University Press, 2005.

Woodward, S. C. "Assessing Young Children's Musical Understanding." *Music Education International* 40 (2002): 112–21.

Woodward, S. C. "Musical Origins." *Sound Ideas* 3, no. 1 (1999): 7–13.

Woodward, S. C., and F. Guidozzi. "Intrauterine Rhythm and Blues?" *British Journal of Obstetrics and Gynaecology* 99 (1992): 787–90.

Zatorre, R. J. "The Biological Foundations of Music." Robert J. Zatorre and Isabelle Peretz, eds. *Annals of the New York Academy of Sciences* 930 (2001).

Zatorre, R., and A. Blood. "Music's Gut Reaction." *Science* 294, no. 5541 (October 12, 2001): 297. doi:10.1126/science.294.5541.297a.

Zatorre, R. J. "The Biological Foundations of Music." Robert J. Zatorre and Isabelle Peretz, eds. *Annals of the New York Academy of Sciences* 930 (2001).

Zatorre, R. J. "Music, the Food of Neuroscience?" *Nature* 434 (2005): 312–15.

INDEX

A NOTE ON THE AUTHOR

Elena Mannes has won six Emmys and many other national awards for her documentaries. She is a member of one of the first families of American music. Her grandparents founded the Mannes College of Music in New York City, and her great uncle, Walter Damrosch, conducted the Metropolitan Opera and was the instigator for the building of Carnegie Hall.